Legalines®

Editorial Advisors:
Gloria A. Aluise
Attorney at Law
Jonathan Neville
Attorney at Law
Robert A. Wyler
Attorney at Law

Authors:
Gloria A. Aluise
Attorney at Law
Daniel O. Bernstine
Attorney at Law
Roy L. Brooks
Professor of Law
Scott M. Burbank
C.P.A.
Charles N. Carnes
Professor of Law
Paul S. Dempsey
Professor of Law
Jerome A. Hoffman
Professor of Law
Mark R. Lee
Professor of Law
Jonathan Neville
Attorney at Law
Laurence C. Nolan
Professor of Law
Arpiar Saunders
Attorney at Law
Robert A. Wyler
Attorney at Law

D1309214

INCOME TAX

Adaptable to Fifteenth Edition* of Klein Casebook

By Scott M. Burbank
C.P.A.

*If your casebook is a newer edition, go to www.gilbertlaw.com
to see if a supplement is available for this title.

THOMSON
WEST

EDITORIAL OFFICE: 1 N. Dearborn Street, Suite 650, Chicago, IL 60602
REGIONAL OFFICES: Chicago, Dallas, Los Angeles, New York, Washington, D.C.

SERIES EDITOR
Linda C. Schneider, J.D.
Attorney at Law

PRODUCTION MANAGER
Elizabeth G. Duke

FIRST PRINTING—2010

Legalines®

**Features Detailed Briefs of Every Major Case,
Plus Summaries of the Black Letter Law**

Titles Available

Administrative Law .... Keyed to Breyer
Administrative Law .... Keyed to Schwartz
Administrative Law .... Keyed to Strauss
Antitrust .... Keyed to Areeda
Antitrust .... Keyed to Pitofsky
Business Associations .... Keyed to Klein
Civil Procedure .... Keyed to Friedenthal
Civil Procedure .... Keyed to Hazard
Civil Procedure .... Keyed to Yeazell
Conflict of Laws .... Keyed to Currie
Constitutional Law .... Keyed to Brest
Constitutional Law .... Keyed to Choper
Constitutional Law .... Keyed to Cohen
Constitutional Law .... Keyed to Rotunda
Constitutional Law .... Keyed to Stone
Constitutional Law .... Keyed to Sullivan
Contracts .... Keyed to Calamari
Contracts .... Keyed to Dawson
Contracts .... Keyed to Farnsworth
Contracts .... Keyed to Fuller
Contracts .... Keyed to Kessler
Contracts .... Keyed to Knapp
Contracts .... Keyed to Murphy
Corporations .... Keyed to Choper
Corporations .... Keyed to Eisenberg
Corporations .... Keyed to Hamilton

Criminal Law .... Keyed to Dressler
Criminal Law .... Keyed to Johnson
Criminal Law .... Keyed to Kadish
Criminal Law .... Keyed to Kaplan
Criminal Law .... Keyed to LaFave
Criminal Procedure .... Keyed to Kamisar
Domestic Relations .... Keyed to Wadlington
Estates and Trusts .... Keyed to Dobris
Evidence .... Keyed to Mueller
Evidence .... Keyed to Waltz
Family Law .... Keyed to Areen
Income Tax .... Keyed to Freeland
Income Tax .... Keyed to Klein
Labor Law .... Keyed to Cox
Property .... Keyed to Cribbet
Property .... Keyed to Dukeminier
Property .... Keyed to Nelson
Property .... Keyed to Rabin
Remedies .... Keyed to Rendelman
Securities Regulation .... Keyed to Coffee
Torts .... Keyed to Dobbs
Torts .... Keyed to Epstein
Torts .... Keyed to Franklin
Torts .... Keyed to Henderson
Torts .... Keyed to Prosser
Wills, Trusts & Estates .... Keyed to Dukeminier

All Titles Available at Your Law School Bookstore

THOMSON

WEST

SHORT SUMMARY OF CONTENTS

TABLE OF CONTENTS AND SHORT REVIEW OUTLINE

I. INTRODUCTION

A. TAX RATES

The tax tables and rate schedules used to compute the federal income tax are progressive; *i.e.*, the rate increases as taxable income increases.

1. **Individuals.** In the past, individuals were taxed under a structure characterized by many tax brackets and a large difference between the highest and lowest rates. The Tax Reform Act of 1986 reduced the number of tax brackets to two. The rate brackets were 15% and 28%. In 1991, a third tax bracket was added, and two more brackets were added in 1993. The Economic Growth and Tax Relief Reconciliation Act of 2001 added yet another tax bracket and an overall reduction in the tax rates to be phased in over a number of years. For 2008, the rates for married taxpayers filing jointly are as follows:

Taxable Income	Rate
$ 0 to $ 16,050	10%
$ 16,050 to $ 65,100	15%
$ 65,100 to $131,450	25%
$131,450 to $200,300	28%
$200,300 to $357,700	33%
$357,700 and above	35%

2. **Corporations**. The 2008 tax rates for corporations are as follows:

Taxable Income	Rate
$ 0 to $ 50,000	15%
$ 50,000 to $ 75,000	25%
$ 75,000 to $ 100,000	34%
$ 100,000 to $ 335,000	39%
$ 335,000 to $10,000,000	34%
$10,000,000 to $15,000,000	35%
$15,000,000 to $18,333,333	38%
$18,333,333 and above	35%

    The corporate rate schedule neutralizes the benefit of the two lowest brackets for higher-income corporations by levying a 5% surtax on corporate taxable income between $100,001 and $335,000. Corporations that pay tax at the corporate level (C corporations) with taxable incomes of at least $335,001 but not over $10 million essentially pay a flat 34% tax. Taxable income over $10 million is taxed at 35%, but with a surtax of the lesser of $100,000 or 3% of taxable income over $15 million. Above $18,333,333, the tax rate becomes a flat 35%. Corporations that have made an S election generally are not taxed as corporations. Instead, their net income passes through and is taxed directly to the shareholders on their personal income tax returns. Certain personal service corporations are taxed at a flat rate of 35%, regardless of the amount of their taxable income.

B. PROCEDURE AND ADMINISTRATION

1. **Filing the Tax Return.** The federal tax system requires taxpayers to make their own determination of their tax liability. Most individuals file returns (form 1040, 1040A, or 1040EZ) on a calendar year basis and must file by April 15 of the following year. However, in many cases, the taxpayer's liability has already been paid by his employer by withholding a portion of the taxpayer's income and depositing the amount with the government. At year's end, the employer is required to give all employees a statement of their individual wages withheld and paid (form W-2). Individuals who receive their income from other sources, such as interest or dividends, are not subject to withholding laws. Therefore, they must estimate their taxable income and pay their estimated tax liability in quarterly installments. Individuals who do not comply may be subject to interest and penalty charges.

2. **Internal Revenue Service (IRS) Review of Returns.** The review of taxpayers' returns begins with a check for mathematical errors. All returns are then subjected to a computer screening process which identifies returns that have a likelihood of audit adjustments. This process tends to select corporate tax returns and individual income tax returns with high income, large deductions, or some other deviation from the statistical norm. The specific criteria which govern whether a return will be audited are carefully guarded by the Service. Generally, the IRS has only three years from the time the return is filed to assess additional tax.

3. **The Audit and Administrative Appeals Procedure.** An audit can take one of three forms. In a "correspondence audit," the taxpayer is asked to mail specific information to the IRS. An "office audit" requires the taxpayer to appear at the district director's office. In a "field audit," the IRS official examines the taxpayer's books and materials at his place of business. If the audit is conducted by a "special agent" rather than a "revenue agent," a civil penalty assessment or criminal charge may be in the offing. If the taxpayer and agent cannot resolve their differences, the taxpayer is given a "30-day letter" which gives him that amount of time to appeal to the district director. If the taxpayer chooses, he may disregard the 30-day letter and petition the Tax Court.

    a. **Administrative reviews.** The district and appellate offices offer an informal appeal process whereby the taxpayer, with or without counsel, is given an opportunity to air his side of the case. Most cases heard here are resolved. If a dispute remains, the taxpayer may take his appeal from the district office to the appellate division. If the administrative procedure is exhausted without resolution, the taxpayer has three avenues of judicial recourse.

b. **Judicial review.** An appeal is usually filed with the Tax Court, which stays any tax assessment. A review can also be brought, after payment of the disputed deficiency, to the district court or the United States Claims Court.

C. CONSTITUTIONAL HISTORY

1. **Pre-Sixteenth Amendment Years.** Before 1913, the federal government used the taxing power for the singular purpose of raising revenues, particularly in time of war. The power to tax was limited by Article I, section 9 of the Constitution, which required that any *direct* tax be apportioned to the various states according to each state's population. The first income tax was held unconstitutional as an *unapportioned* direct tax in *Pollock v. Farmers' Loan & Trust Co.,* 157 U.S. 429 (1895). During those years, taxes and tariffs on alcohol, tobacco, and real estate predominated.

2. **Sixteenth Amendment.** The Sixteenth Amendment took effect in 1913 and gave Congress the power to impose income taxes without regard to apportionment.

3. **Recent History.** Since 1913, the income tax has not been used solely as a device to collect revenues. Instead, the revenue acts have been designed to stimulate capital formation, serve special interest groups, stabilize the economy, reduce deficits, and increase the "equity" in the system. These and other social objectives have resulted in the increased complexity and apparent inequity of the current tax system.

4. **Present Federal Tax Law.** Until enactment of the Tax Reform Act of 1986, the body of federal tax law was referred to as the Internal Revenue Code of 1954, as amended. However, because the 1986 amendments were so substantial, the current body of federal tax law is now referred to as the Internal Revenue Code of 1986. The income tax is one of more than 50 different taxes imposed by this statute.

D. SOURCES OF FEDERAL INCOME TAX LAW

Federal tax law is based principally on statutes rather than common law.

1. **Internal Revenue Code of 1986 (I.R.C.).** Title 26 of the United States Code (U.S.C.) is the primary source of authority for federal tax law.

2. **Treasury Regulations.** Regulations are drafted by the United States Treasury Department under authority from Congress.

   a. **Legislative.** The regulations are drafted to cover specific provisions of the Code. They carry the force of law unless they are drafted too broadly so as to fall outside of their specific mandate.

   b. **Interpretive.** Some regulations are interpretive. They are issued under general authority granted by Congress. These are given a strong presumption of correctness by the courts.

3. **Revenue Rulings and Procedures.** These are written by IRS attorneys and are not official pronouncements. They respond to a limited factual setting; therefore, their scope is limited.

4. **Rulings and Determination Letters.** These are written to taxpayers' inquiries sent to the IRS national office or a district director. These are issued only if a clear determination can be made from the Code, a treasury regulation, or a court decision.

5. **Judicial Opinions.** Tax controversies are heard by the United States Supreme Court, courts of appeals, district courts, and the United States Claims Court. In addition, the United States Tax Court is specifically set aside for this purpose.

E. INTRODUCTION TO INCOME TAX TERMINOLOGY

1. **Tax Computation.** The formula for computing individual income tax is as follows:

Gross income [I.R.C.§61]
   minus: *Business expenses* [I.R.C §62]
   equals: *Adjusted gross income.*

Adjusted gross income
   minus: *Personal exemptions* and either the *standard deduction* or *itemized deductions*
   equals: *Taxable income.*

Taxable income
   times: *Tax rate*
   equals: *Tax due on taxable income.*

Tax due on taxable income
   minus: *Credits*
   equals: *Tax due.*

2. **Capital Gain.** As will be shown later in this outline, capital gain or loss is gain or loss from the "sale or exchange of a capital asset." A capital asset is statutorily defined as "property," with a number of exceptions that include inventory, property held by the taxpayer primarily for sale to customers in the ordinary course of his business or trade, and other limited exceptions. The Tax Reform Act of 1986 eliminated preferential tax rate treatment for capital gains. The Taxpayer Relief Act of 1997 reinstated preferential tax rates for long-term capital gains, assessing a maximum tax rate of 15% for individuals, estates, and trusts. The tax laws related to the area of capital gains are numerous and complex.

3. **Tax Accounting.** Normal accounting rules are followed generally for tax purposes. The two basic methods of tax accounting are the "cash receipts and disbursements" method (or "cash" method) and the "accrual" method. Under the cash method, amounts are treated as income when received in cash (or cash equivalents) and are deductible when paid. Under the accrual method, items are included in gross income when earned regardless of when payment is actually received, and items of expense are deducted when the obligation to pay is incurred, again regardless of when payment is made. Corporate taxpayers with gross receipts in excess of $5 million are not allowed to use the cash method of accounting.

4. **Realization and Recognition.** A gain or loss is said to be realized when there has been some change in circumstances such that the gain or loss might be taken into account for tax purposes. A gain realized is then said to be *recognized* when the change in circumstances is such that the gain or loss is actually taken into account. Therefore, a realization of gain does not necessarily bring forth immediate gain recognition. This is true in the case of asset appreciation.

   a. **Example.** If a capital asset is purchased for $20,000, and over the course of a five-year period it appreciates to $50,000, then gain has been realized in the amount of $30,000. However, this gain would not be recognized until the asset is sold or otherwise disposed of. At this point in time, recognition would occur.

5. **Depreciation and Cost Recovery.** Generally accepted accounting principles and basic tax accounting require the matching of expenses with revenues derived from such expenses. This "matching principle" precludes the current expensing of assets that benefit future periods.

   a. **Example.** Suppose a taxpayer purchases a machine which will produce inventory items that will be held for sale over a 20-year period. Even though the expense for the machinery has been realized or paid in the first year of operation, the matching principle requires that the cost of the machinery be spread over the 20-year period when revenues will be realized from its production. To recover this investment, the taxpayer takes a deduction traditionally called depreciation. Congress now terms depreciation as ACRS or the Accelerated Cost Recovery System. In any event, the principle is that the cost of the income-producing asset will be spread over its productive life. This will be explained in greater detail later in the outline.

6. **Entities.**

a. **Proprietor.** This is a person who owns a business directly without partners or co-owners. All items of income and expense are treated as those of the proprietor himself.

b. **Partnership.** This is a combination of two or more people who have agreed to carry on a business for profit. Although the partnership files a tax return, it is a conduit for information purposes only, since items of income and expense flow through to the partners themselves.

c. **Trust.** This is a device where a trustee holds and invests property for the benefit of another person. Generally, income and expense of the trust flow through to the beneficiary. However, in some circumstances, the trust is required to pay the income taxes.

d. **Corporations.** Unlike a partnership, a corporation is treated as a separate entity from its owners. The corporation computes its income tax and makes a payment of tax on the net profit earned. In addition, payments of income from the corporation to its shareholders are called dividends. These are taxed to the individual shareholders. In this regard, income is taxed twice when earned by a corporation.

e. **S-Corporations.** An S-Corporation is a regular corporation formed under state law. However, for federal tax purposes its shareholders are taxed in a manner similar to partners in a partnership. Note, however, that some states do not recognize this special tax treatment for purposes of state tax laws.

f. **Limited liability company.** A limited liability company is a relatively new form of business entity that limits members' liability, yet is treated as a partnership for income tax purposes.

F. DEFERRAL AND ITS VALUE

It is generally understood that a dollar today is worth more than a dollar obtained in the future. This is due to the "time value of money" and is based on the notion that a dollar that is used today or invested is worth more than it could be when received in the future. The opposite is true for payments of expenses, such as income taxes. Thus, a taxpayer who can defer the payment of taxes obtains the interim benefit of using the taxes that would otherwise have been paid currently. For this reason, a common taxpayer strategy is not only the avoidance of tax, but also its deferral. Many transactions, such as like-kind exchanges (which will be discussed in greater detail, *infra*) are utilized solely for their deferral benefit. In fact, this concept is the basis of most legitimate tax shelters.

II. SOME CHARACTERISTICS OF INCOME

A. INTRODUCTION

I.R.C. section 61 defines gross income as "all income from whatever source derived." Compensation for services, rents, royalties, interest, and dividends are explicitly included. Sections 71 to 83 mention additional items that are included. Sections 101 to 123 specifically exclude other items from gross income.

B. THEORIES OF INCOME

1. **The Simons Definition.** Income is the sum of the market value of rights exercised in consumption and the change in value of property rights between the beginning and the end of a period. Thus $I = C + (EV - BV)$. This definition is broader than the income tax definition.

2. **Increase in Net Worth.** A common definition of income is that any item which increases a taxpayer's net worth is gross income. [Commissioner v. Glenshaw Glass Co., 348 U.S. 426 (1955)] Thus, any increment in net worth is presumed to be income, unless it is specifically excluded.

    a. **Repayment of a loan.** Repayment of a loan does not bring the lender income. This is merely a change in the form of property from that of a receivable to cash. However, interest received on the loan is income.

    b. **Borrowing money.** Borrowing money does not produce income since liabilities have increased along with assets, leaving net worth the same as before.

    c. **Noncash receipts.** Noncash receipts may be income even if the benefit is in the form of property or services.

    d. **Unsolicited property.** Unsolicited property (*e.g.*, property received in the mail) is not income unless there is an intent to retain the property or some associated benefit is shown.

3. **Gain from Capital, Labor, or Both.** A narrow definition of income is that income results from any gain attributed to the taxpayer's capital or labor. [Eisner v. Macomber, 252 U.S. 189 (1920)] The present law can best be understood as an evolution of this narrow definition.

C. NONCASH BENEFITS

1. **Introduction.** One can receive income in forms other than money; *e.g.*, property (real or personal) that is convertible into money. "Income" also includes noncash benefits that are not convertible into money. For example, a corporation provides a house or an automobile for an executive's personal use.

2. **Food and Lodging Supplied to Employees.**

   a. **"Convenience of employer" test--**

Benaglia v. Commissioner, 36 B.T.A. 838 (1937).

Facts. Benaglia (P), a resort hotel manager, was required to be available at all times to handle any emergency. Implicit in P's employment contract was that he was to eat and sleep at the hotel. The Commissioner (D) assessed a tax deficiency, claiming that the meals and lodging were includable in P's gross income.

Issue. If meals and lodging are given for the employer's convenience, should the employee be taxed for these benefits?

Held. No. Judgment for P.

♦ When benefits are imposed on an employee for the employer's benefit, the employee should not be taxed for them. The value of the meals and lodging received by P was an implicit part of P's obligation for the convenience of his employer and should be received tax free.

Dissent. P's meals and lodging were intended to be compensation that gave him an economic benefit.

Comment. According to I.R.C. section 119, if an employee is required to live on the premises or to take meals there, then there is no income. Convenience of the employer exists when there is "a substantial noncompensatory, business reason" served by having the employee on the premises.

---

   b. **Business premises requirement.** The meals or lodging must be furnished on the business premises of the employer. And, in the case of lodging, it must be accepted as a condition of employment (*e.g.*, meals and quarters furnished to firemen at the station house).

   c. **Business necessity test.** In *Commissioner v. Kowalski,* 434 U.S. 77 (1977), the Supreme Court suggested that convenience of the employer means "business necessity"; *i.e.*, that the job could not be performed unless meals or lodging were supplied.

  d. **Cash reimbursements.** Note that section 119 does not only cover meals and lodging furnished in kind. Amounts paid in cash to the employee for meals and lodging are also excluded from income. [Treas. Reg. 1.119-1(f), example 3]

  e. **Payment for injury or sickness.**

    1) **Health and accident insurance.** Premiums paid by the employer are not included in the employee's gross income.

    2) **Sick pay.** Amounts paid directly to the employee are excluded, depending on hospitalization, absence, and amount of sick pay as compared to the employee's regular wages. The exclusion does not apply to the extent that the employee's adjusted gross income exceeds $15,000.

 3. **Other Fringe Benefits.** In 1984, a comprehensive set of rules covering fringe benefits was enacted. [I.R.C. §132] The rules outline types of fringe benefits that are excluded from gross income.

  a. **No additional cost service.** The entire value of any "no additional cost" service provided to an employee is excluded from gross income (for example, free travel for airline employees).

  b. **Qualified employee discounts.** Employee discounts offered to employees on a nondiscriminatory basis are excluded from the employee's gross income. However, the amount of the discount cannot exceed 20% of the selling price.

  c. **Working condition fringe.** The value of property or services provided to employees is excluded to the extent that the costs would otherwise have been deductible had the employee paid for the property or service.

  d. **De minimis fringes.** The value of small fringe benefits that would be impracticable to administer but which would otherwise be taxed are excluded from gross income. Examples of these would include special event tickets, coffee, cocktail parties, etc.

  e. **Qualified tuition reduction.** College tuition reduction for, *e.g.*, the children of a faculty member of the college is excluded.

  f. **Other special rules.** Special rules are provided for athletic facilities, parking or eating facilities, luxury autos, etc.

4. Another Approach to Valuation--

Turner v. Commissioner, 13 T.C.M. 462 (1954).

Facts. The taxpayer (P) participated in a local radio contest in which he won two round-trip first-class steamship tickets for a cruise between New York City and Buenos Aires. The price to purchase two comparable first-class tickets would have been $2,220. The tickets were not transferable and there were restrictions on their use. P surrendered his rights to the two first-class tickets with an additional $12.50 in exchange for four round-trip tourist steamship tickets between New York City and P's wife's homeland of Brazil. The Commissioner (D) claims that P should have reported $2,220 as taxable income from winning the contest. P reported a value of $520 on his 1948 tax return.

Issue. Was the taxable value of the prize $2,220?

Held. No.

♦   The taxable value of the prize is $1,400, which is in between the amounts claimed by P and D. P would not have purchased such luxury items, and if P had tried to sell the tickets he would have had to discount the price of the tickets and would also have incurred selling expenses. However, P did benefit significantly by being able to take his family on a cruise as well as by saving living expenses while on the trip. The court must arrive at some figure and has done so.

D. IMPUTED INCOME

1.   **Definition.** Imputed income is created when a taxpayer works for or uses her property for her own benefit. If a taxpayer lives in her own house, she theoretically is paying herself rental income. Also, a homemaker receives imputed income for domestic services rendered in her own home. Congress generally has not sought to tax imputed income.

2.   **Working for Yourself.** In *Commissioner v. Miner,* 279 F.2d 338 (5th Cir. 1960), the taxpayer, an insurance agent, sold himself policies. The court held that the benefits from labor on his own behalf constituted income. In *Benjamin v. Hoey,* 139 F.2d 945 (2d Cir. 1944), a partner in a brokerage firm received commissions for transactions on his own account, which were held *not* to be income. The courts have been rather inconsistent in this area. In the Second Circuit, products of a farm consumed by a farmer were held excludable from income, while the Tax Court has held a store owner's consumption of groceries to be income to him.

3. **Homemakers.** If two homemakers did each other's work for pay, the taxable income is greater than if each does her own work. Also, there are many cases where the spouse takes a job and employs a servant to do the work she formerly did. However, the spouse's employment increases the family's income only by the amount her earnings exceed the wages paid the servant.

4. **Exchanges of Goods and Services.**

   a. **Introduction.** Many times taxpayers will avoid payment of cash for goods or services (and its associated taxability) by exchanging goods or services for the benefit received.

   b. **Administrative responses.** In Rev. Rul. 79-24, 1979-1 C.B. 60, the IRS stated that if services are paid for in a method other than in money, the fair market value of the property or services taken in payment must be included in income. If the services were rendered at a stipulated price, such price will be presumed to be the fair market value of the compensation received, in the absence of evidence to the contrary. (This is quoted from Treas. Reg. section 1.61.2(d)(1).)

   c. **Example.** In return for personal legal services performed by a lawyer for a house painter, the latter painted the lawyer's personal residence. The fair market value of the services received by the lawyer and the house painter are included in their respective gross incomes under section 61 of the Code.

   d. **Example.** If a landlord receives a work of art by her artist-tenant in return for rent-free use of an apartment for six months, the fair market value of the work of art and the six months' rental value of the apartment must be included in each party's gross income.

E. WINDFALLS AND GIFTS

1. **Damages.**

   a. **Introduction.** Damage awards or settlements are generally thought to be compensatory for either personal injury or a return of business capital and are thus not includable as taxable gain. [I.R.C. §104]

   b. **Punitive damages--**

Commissioner v. Glenshaw Glass Co., 348 U.S. 426 (1955).

Facts. Two cases with similar factual backgrounds were decided here. Glenshaw Glass (P) sued a machinery supplier for fraud and antitrust violations. P obtained a judgment of $800,000, $325,000 of which represented punitive damages. In the other action,

William Goldman Theatres, Inc. (P) won an antitrust judgment of $375,000, $125,000 of which represented lost profits. The remainder constituted punitive damages. Neither plaintiff reported the punitive damages as income and the Commissioner (D) made deficiency assessments. D appeals from judgments for Ps.

Issue. Are damage awards which are not compensatory in nature income to the recipient?

Held. Yes. Decision of Board of Tax Appeals is reversed.

♦ Congress has not applied limitations to the gross income concept due to the nature of the receipt. The Court has given a liberal construction to the phrase "gross income."

♦ The mere fact that the payments were extracted from the wrongdoer as punishment does not detract from their character as taxable income to the recipient. It would be anomalous to concede that compensatory damages are income but punitive damages, which are clear gains in net worth, are not.

Comment. To determine taxability, the nature of the compensation must be determined. For example, compensatory damages for lost profits or punitive damages are taxable as income, but damages given as reimbursement for lost capital is not recognizable as income. In limited circumstances, I.R.C. section 186 allows a deduction to offset damages received in cases involving antitrust violations.

---

2. **Gifts vs. Income—The Basic Concept.**

   a. **Introduction.** I.R.C. section 102 excludes from gross income "the value of property acquired by gift, bequest, devise, or inheritance." *Example:* A transfers Blackacre to B when its basis is $1,000 and its fair market value is $2,000. Under our present system A has no gain and B has no present gain.

   b. **Definition.** The primary motive of the donor determines if the transaction is made because of "detached and disinterested generosity" and is therefore a gift (not deductible as an expense to the donor and not includable as income to the recipient). This definition is applied by the courts to restrict many would-be "gifts."

3. **Payment for Referrals--**

Commissioner v. Duberstein; Stanton v. United States, 363 U.S. 278 (1960).

Facts. Duberstein (P) referred customers to Berman, which United States proved to be profitable to Berman. Though Duberstein did not expect payment, Berman gave him a Cadillac. Berman deducted the price of the car as a business expense. Duberstein did not include the Cadillac as income. Stanton (P) was the controller of a church. When he resigned, the church's board voted him a "gratuity" of $20,000. Stanton had no enforceable right to or claim for the payment. He did not include the $20,000 in his income. The car and the money were held to be gifts to Ps and therefore not includable in their income. The Commissioner (D) appeals.

Issue. Were Duberstein's car and Stanton's money given to them with a "detached and disinterested generosity" so as to constitute gifts?

Held. No. The court of appeals' decision in *Duberstein* is reversed. The court of appeals' decision in *Stanton* is vacated and remanded to the district court.

♦ Where the payment is in return for services rendered, it is irrelevant that the donor derives no economic benefit from it. It is not a gift—it is income. Here, Duberstein and Stanton rendered services.

♦ The mere absence of a legal or moral duty to make such a payment, or the lack of economic incentive to do so, does not in itself show a gift.

♦ Whether a transfer amounts to a gift depends upon consideration of all of the facts surrounding the transfer. The trier of fact should be given discretion in determining the donor's intent.

Concurrence (Whittaker, J.). Whether a transfer is a gift is a mixed question of law and fact.

Dissent (Douglas, J.). A presumption should exist that a transfer is of a business nature if the donee has rendered services. The two transactions constituted gifts.

Comment. A gift exists if it "proceeds from a detached and disinterested generosity, out of affection, respect, admiration, charity, or like impulses." Here, the Court found that the monies were given for services rendered.

---

4. **Payments to Mistresses--**

United States v. Harris, 942 F.2d 1125 (7th Cir. 1991).

Facts. David Kritzik directly or indirectly gave Conley and Harris, twin sisters, each more than half a million dollars over a period of several years. After Kritzik's death, Conley and Harris (Ds) were convicted of willfully evading their income tax obligations by not having claimed amounts received from Kritzik as taxable income. Ds appeal.

Issue. Are amounts received by taxpayers during long-term personal relationships taxable income to the recipients?

Held. No. Convictions reversed.

♦   A person is entitled to treat items received from a lover as gifts as long as the relationship consists of "something more than specific payments for specific sessions of sex."

♦   This is a criminal tax case. To be found guilty, Ds must be shown to have violated a clear rule of law. The government was unable to show clear evidence that Kritzik did not have a donative intent in transferring property to Ds. In addition, the prior court cases covering payments to mistresses do not provide a clear rule of law that could subject Ds to criminal prosecution.

---

5.   **Bargain Purchases.** Whether a taxpayer's purchase of property for a bargain price is a gift or income depends on the motive of the seller and all of the surrounding circumstances. For example, if an automobile dealer allows certain employees to purchase cars at below the market price as an employment benefit, the bargain element is income to the employee. Here, the benefit is given as compensation rather than as a gift.

6.   **Dealers' "Tokes."** In *Olk v. United States*, 536 F.2d 876 (9th Cir.), *cert. denied,* 429 U.S. 920 (1976), the Ninth Circuit determined that "tokes," gifts given to dealers by gamblers, were not gifts. These "tokes" are not motivated by detached and disinterested generosity. They are motivated by an intensely interested act, accompanied by impulsiveness and superstition. Generally, receipts must meet certain conditions to be taxable income. One, the taxpayer must be engaged in rendering a service. Two, the contributor of the receipt and the taxpayer must have personal or functional contact in the course of performing these services. Tokes, like tips, meet these conditions.

7.   **Prizes, Awards, Scholarships, and Fellowships.**

a.   **Prizes and awards.** Prior law allowed a limited exclusion from income for awards or prizes in recognition of religious, charitable, or educational accomplishment. Under the 1986 Act, all such awards will be included in income except where the recipient assigns the award to a governmental unit or tax-exempt organization.

b.   **Scholarships and fellowships.**

1) **Introduction.** Prior to the Tax Reform Act of 1986, amounts received for scholarships and fellowships were excluded from gross income. In addition, if the degree candidates were required to perform services as a part of obtaining the scholarship, the income attributable to such services was taxable. However if such services were required of all degree candidates, the entire scholarship was nontaxable.

2) **Changes in the law.** The Tax Reform Act of 1986 modified the prior law and allows only limited exclusions. The exclusion is limited to degree candidates. In addition, the scholarship must be used for tuition, fees, books, supplies, and for equipment required for specific courses. The 1986 law retains the provisions related to the taxability of payments for services, but repealed the exception for services required of all candidates.

3) **Students not working for educational degrees.** For nondegree candidates, grants are included in gross income *unless* the grantor is a charitable organization, university, or the government.

8. **Transfer of Unrealized Gain.**

   a. **Basis carried over to donee--**

Taft v. Bowers, 278 U.S. 470 (1929).

Facts. Taft (P) was given stock from her father, which she later sold. The Commissioner (D) assessed P a tax based on the difference between the donor's cost and the amount realized by the donee. This case and a companion case were illustrated by the Court as follows: A purchased 100 shares of stock for $1,000. Five years later, when the stock was worth $2,000, A gave the shares to B. B later sold the stock for $5,000. B maintains that she should be taxed on only $3,000, *i.e.*, the gain during her ownership. The Service claims that B must recognize a gain of $4,000 for the total appreciation from the time A acquired the stock until B sold it.

Issue. When someone receives property as a gift, is the donor's basis carried over to the donee (for purposes of gain recognition when the donee later sells the property)?

Held. Yes. Judgment affirmed.

♦   Clearly, Congress intended to tax the entire profit from the time of the donor's acquisition to the time of the donee's sale of the property.

♦   There is nothing in the Constitution that limits the application of tax to only the appreciation that occurs while the property is in the possession of the donee-seller.

Comment. Gifts are not taxed as income to the recipient. The donee assumes the donor's basis in the gifted property, increased by the amount of gift taxes paid by the donor (up to the fair market value of the property).

---

b. **Basis.** As the previous case illustrates, for purposes of computing gain and depreciation, the donee takes the donor's basis in the gifted property. For purposes of computing loss, I.R.C. section 1015 requires the donee's basis to be the lower of the donor's basis or the fair market value of the property at the date of the gift.

c. **Holding period.** Section 1223(2) states that a donee of property is entitled to "tack" the holding period of the donor to the period of time when the property is held by the donee if the property has the same basis "in whole or in part" in the donee's and donor's hands. This is important in determining whether property disposed of by the donee qualifies for long-term capital gain treatment (*see* VIII, *infra*).

d. **Bargain sales.** Suppose A's father transfers property with a $30 basis and worth $100 to his son for $40. Treas. Reg. section 1.1015-4 states that the father should recognize a gain of $10, while the son would have a $40 basis.

e. **Transfers at death**. Section 1014 provides that the basis of property acquired by reason of death is the fair market value at the date of death or, at the administrator's/executor's election under section 2032, at the optional valuation date; *i.e.*, six months after death.

f. **Gifts of divided interest**. Some gifts are given in increments; *e.g.*, a grandparent leaves a certificate of deposit to his son for the benefit of his grandson, requiring that the annual interest be used for the child's benefit until the CD expires. Upon expiration of the CD, the principal is turned over to the grandson. The income is taxable under sections 102(b) and 273. The gift of principal is not taxable to the grandson.

F. RECOVERY OF CAPITAL

1. **Introduction.** Income includes the production of any asset. This includes interest, rents, dividends, and other returns on the cost of the investment. Income also includes the gain from the sale or other final disposition of the asset. However, it does not include the return or recovery of the cost of the asset. For example, if land is purchased for $100,000, and later sold for the same amount, no taxable gain would be recognized by the taxpayer. This would be an example of a return or recovery of the cost of an asset.

2. **Sales of Easements--**

Inaja Land Co. v. Commissioner, 9 T.C. 727 (1947).

Facts. Inaja (P) owned a fishing lake that became polluted due to the construction of a tunnel. P was paid $50,000 from the city for the release of all liability. The Commissioner (D) taxed P for a portion of the $50,000, which he said represented income.

Issue. When real property has been damaged, should a recovery that is less than the land's basis be taxable?

Held. No. Judgment for P.

♦ Here the proceeds could not be apportioned between the real estate and an easement which P also held. When no apportionment can be made, no tax liability exists until the entire cost of capital has been recovered. Since the recovery here was less than P's basis in the land, it must be considered a return of capital.

Comment. Treas. Reg. section 1.61-6 states that on a sale of subdivided property, gain or loss shall be computed on the sale of each parcel, notwithstanding that the taxpayer has not recouped his entire investment. What if A pays $10,000 for a 10-acre tract of land and then sells a one-half undivided interest in it for $7,000. Income? Yes. Allocate the basis in accordance with the fair market value at the date of purchase.

---

3. **Life Insurance.**

   a. **Introduction.** Benefits paid on a life insurance policy by reason of the insured's death are not taxable. [I.R.C. §101] This is true regardless of who paid the premiums on the policy. For example, a payment of insurance proceeds to a stockholder on a policy paid for by a corporation is not taxed as a dividend to the beneficiary-stockholder.

   b. **Installment payments.** If insurance proceeds are paid in installments rather than in a lump sum, the interest portion of the installments is taxable income to the beneficiary. This is addressed in section 101(c) of the Code.

      1) **Relief for surviving spouse.** A surviving spouse beneficiary is given some relief from these provisions. Death benefits paid by the insured's employer are entitled to a limited exemption from income of $5,000 provided by I.R.C. section 101(b).

   c. **Group life insurance.** Generally, the value of life insurance coverage up to $50,000 is excluded from an employee's income. However, starting in 1984, the value of group term life insurance is included in the gross income of certain key employees unless the plan provides benefits on a nondiscriminatory basis. [I.R.C. §79(d)]

4.   Annuities and Pensions.

   a.   Definition. An annuity is an investment which is paid back, with interest, over a set period of time or for the recipient's life. The part of each payment which is a return of the taxpayer's investment is not taxed. The interest portion of the annuity payments, however, is taxable income. [*See* I.R.C. §72] For example, if A invests in a program that pays him $100 per month for life beginning after he reaches the age of 65, he has invested in an annuity.

   b.   Treatment. Determining the nontaxable return-of-capital portion is done by determining the exclusion ratio. I.R.C. section 72(b) defines the exclusion ratio as the cost of the annuity divided by the expected return. The expected return is calculated by either a fixed contract or by reference to life expectancy of the investor. This is determined from actuarial tables (for example, in the case above, the taxpayer's life expectancy at age 65 would be five years). The amount excluded from each payment is the product of the exclusion ratio and the payment. The amount of each payment that exceeds this return-of-capital portion is then taxed as net income. Note that certain employee pension plans that work quite similarly to annuities are treated differently.

   c.   Penalties. There is a 10% penalty tax imposed on premature distributions. In addition, income must be recognized when a taxpayer receives a loan against an annuity policy.

5.   Gains and Losses from Gambling.

   a.   The basic rule. All gains realized from gambling are taxable. Losses, however, for professional and amateur gamblers are deductible only to the extent of offsetting gains. [*See* I.R.C. §165(d)]

   b.   Enforcement. Since gambling is a cash business, enforcement is difficult. For large transactions, safeguards exist. Section 3402(q) requires that a race track withhold taxes at a rate of 20%. In addition, information returns (form 1099) are filed with the IRS.

6.   Recovery of Loss.

   a.   Introduction. I.R.C. section 165 permits deductions for losses (as opposed to business "expenses") incurred in connection with a trade or business as well as for certain losses that are "personal" in nature.

   b.   When do losses occur? A loss is generally deductible when it is "realized," or finalized by a completed transaction or event.

1) **Securities.** A loss is sustained when the security *actually* becomes worthless, *not* when the taxpayer believes it to be worthless.

2) **Real property.** A loss deduction is allowed if an identifiable event fixes the worthlessness of the property, or efforts to restore the property prove fruitless.

3) **Decline in value.** A decline in value is *not* enough to claim a loss deduction. A loss must be evidenced by a sale, exchange, theft, abandonment, destruction, or tangible worthlessness. A reasonable possibility of recoupment precludes a loss deduction claim.

c. **Amount of deduction.** The amount of loss deductible is the difference between the value of the property immediately preceding the loss and the value of the property immediately afterwards. The difference in value claimed as a loss cannot exceed the adjusted basis of the property and is reduced by any insurance or other compensation received as a result of the loss. [I.T. 4032, 1950 C.B. 21 (1950)]

d. **Reimbursement of tax loss--**

Clark v. Commissioner, 40 B.T.A. 333 (1939).

Facts. Clark's (P's) tax counsel gave him some bad advice that cost P $19,941 in additional taxes. After P paid his taxes, his counsel reimbursed him for the $19,941. The Commissioner (D) assessed P with a tax deficiency, claiming that P's taxes were paid by a third party, which constituted income to P. P argued that the amount received was compensation for damages or loss caused by the error of the tax counsel.

Issue. Is the reimbursement of unnecessary tax paid due to bad tax advice income to the recipient?

Held. No. Judgment for P.

♦ The $19,941 was paid to P not as a payment of his taxes, but as compensation for his loss. The measure of the loss (or damages) was the sum of money which P became legally obligated to pay because of another's negligence. The fact that the obligation was for taxes is irrelevant.

G. ANNUAL ACCOUNTING AND ITS CONSEQUENCES

1. **Long-Term Contracts--**

Burnet v. Sanford & Brooks Co., 282 U.S. 359 (1931).

Facts. Sanford & Brooks Co. (P) engaged in a long-term dredging contract with another company. P recognized contract payments received each year as income and deducted that year's expense. From 1913 to 1916, expenses exceeded payments by $176,271.88. P's tax returns for 1913, 1915, and 1916 showed net losses. P brought suit in 1916 to recover the losses and in 1920 was awarded $192,577.59, which included the $176,271.88 of losses plus interest. P did not include this award in his 1920 income, and the Commissioner (D) made a deficiency assessment. The court of appeals ruled that only the interest portion should be recognized as income in 1920, and the remainder constituted a return of losses. D appeals.

Issue. Should all money received in a given year be included in gross income for that year?

Held. Yes. Judgment reversed.

♦ All the revenue acts since the adoption of the Sixteenth Amendment have uniformly assessed tax on the basis of annual returns showing the net result of the taxpayer's transactions for that year. The taxpayer is required to include in gross income all items received during the taxable year.

♦ The receipt in 1920 did not any the less constitute net income for that year because P suffered net losses in the previous years equal to the amount received.

♦ The expenses incurred from 1913 to 1916 were for the purpose of earning profits. They were not capital expenditures.

Comment. Treas. Reg. section 1.451.3 provides two special methods of reporting income from long-term contracts. This regulation has great applicability to the construction industry.

Percentage of completion method. This requires the taxpayer to recognize the portion of gross income that corresponds to the percentage of the contract which has been completed. For example, if a taxpayer is under contract to construct a building for $100,000 and he completes one-fifth of it in year one, he will recognize $20,000 of income that year, no matter when it is actually paid.

Completed contract method. This allows the taxpayer to recognize the total gross income from the contract in the year that the entire job is completed. This method has been the subject of much controversy and abuse by some taxpayers.

Current method. The Tax Reform Act of 1986 modified the use of these long-term contract methods. Taxpayers now must use a percentage of completion method that combines the percentage of completion with the old completed contract method. In addition, the rules related to capitalizing costs, determining percentages, etc., have become more complex.

a. **Net Operating Losses (NOL).** The effects of the annual accounting period are somewhat mitigated by the NOL provisions. These rules allow taxpayers to carry losses back three years and forward 15 years.

b. **Mitigation of the statute of limitations.** I.R.C. sections 1311-1314 provide some relief from the harsh effects of the statute of limitations in some cases.

2. **Claim of Right.**

a. **Introduction--**

North American Oil Consolidated v. Burnet, 286 U.S. 417 (1932).

Facts. North American (P) held property owned by the government. A suit was instituted in 1916 and a receiver appointed to manage the property. In 1917, a court held for P and the receiver turned the property's income over to P. The government appealed, and finally lost in 1922. The Commissioner (D) held that the 1916 income should be included in P's 1917 return. The Board of Tax Appeals held the income to be taxable to the receiver in 1916.

Issue. Should impounded funds in the hands of a receiver be taxed to the taxpayer only when an unqualified right exists to receive them?

Held. Yes. Judgment affirmed.

♦ Income could not be taxed to P in 1916 because a receiver held the funds and P might never receive the income. However, in 1917 when the receivership was vacated, P had an unqualified right to the funds. The fact that the suit was not finally settled until 1922 is immaterial. Had P lost, it could have repaid the income and claimed a deduction.

Comment. The Supreme Court explained the claim of right doctrine in this case as follows: "If a taxpayer receives earnings under a claim of right and without restriction as to its disposition, he has received income that he is required to return, even though it may still be claimed that he is not entitled to the money, and even though he may still be adjudged liable to restore its equivalent."

---

b. **Mistaken claims--**

United States v. Lewis, 340 U.S. 590 (1951).

Facts. Lewis (P) received a bonus of $22,000, which he reported on his 1944 return. The bonus was erroneously calculated and P's employer brought suit to recover half of it. In 1946, P lost the suit and repaid $11,000 to his employer. P sought to recompute his 1944 return to reflect an $11,000 bonus. The Commissioner (D) instructed P to claim a loss of $11,000 in 1946. The Court of Claims held that the excess bonus received under a mistake of fact was not income and held for P. D appealed, and the Supreme Court granted certiorari.

Issue. Are earnings which a taxpayer receives under a mistaken claim of right income?

Held. Yes. Judgment reversed.

♦ Nothing in the language of the claim of right rule permits an exception merely because a taxpayer is "mistaken" as to the validity of his claim. The claim of right doctrine has long been used to give finality to the annual accounting period, and is now deeply rooted in the federal tax system.

Dissent (Douglas, J.). The taxpayer should be entitled to a refund of taxes paid in a prior tax year.

Comment. This case and others were materially affected by the passage of I.R.C. section 1341. This statute allows the taxpayer, if the amount exceeds $3,000, to claim the benefit of the deduction in either the earlier or the later year, whichever would be more advantageous to him.

---

c. **Conclusion.** If a taxpayer receives money and property and claims he is entitled to it and can dispose of it, then it is taxable. It is irrelevant that he may have to give the money or property back sometime in the future. (This doctrine is to guard against a taxpayer's "forgetting" to claim income when it is finally received.)

3. **The Tax Benefit Doctrine.**

a. **The basic rule.** Where a deduction in a prior year is followed by a recovery of the item deducted, the recovery constitutes income to the taxpayer in the year received. However, such recovery is taxable only if the previous deduction gave the taxpayer some tax benefit in the prior year.

b. **Codification.** I.R.C. section 111 states: "Gross income does not include income attributable to the recovery during the taxable year of any amount deducted in any prior year to the extent such amount did not reduce income subject to tax." Note that section 111 specifies these consequences only when there is no tax benefit from the deduction; nothing is said about what to do when a tax benefit does in fact exist. So long as the deduction brought a tax benefit, the amount of the tax savings is of no import.

H. RECOVERIES FOR PERSONAL AND BUSINESS INJURIES

1. **Damages for Personal Injuries in General.** Damages compensating an injured person for personal injuries are excludable from gross income under section 104(a)(2). These damages often are excludable even when measured by the amount of wages that could have been earned but for the injuries. Effective for amounts received after August 20, 1996, the exclusion does not apply to nonphysical personal injuries such as age discrimination, injury to reputation, and, in some cases, emotional distress. Punitive damages are taxable as ordinary income, regardless of the underlying physical or non-physical personal injury.

   a. **Status.** *Benaglia v. Commissioner*, *supra*, pointed out the necessity of drawing a line between taxable compensation and nontaxable working conditions. This category of items (*i.e.*, "working conditions") is an aspect of what might be called "status." When status is involuntarily disputed, the damages which a taxpayer receives are a substitute for what he previously enjoyed tax free (*e.g.*, health, privacy, etc.) and are not taxable.

   b. **Voluntary deprivation.** When there is a voluntary deprivation of some element of status—*e.g.*, X sells his blood—then it is income. The tax law is tied to market transactions; here, there is a market.

   c. **A minimum standard of well-being.** Indemnification paid to prisoners of war does not produce income; nor do most payments made by public agencies to individuals (*e.g.*, most Social Security payments and unemployment payments). This reflects a view that certain economic minima are part of the status of citizens as citizens.

   d. **Compensation by insurers.** If the taxpayer receives insurance benefits for which he paid premiums, the benefits are not taxable income. [I.R.C. §104(a)(3)] This is not the case if the taxpayer deducted the premium payments.

2. **Damage to Business Interests.**

   a. **Loss of profits.** Damages recovered for the loss of profits of a business are taxable just as the profit itself would have been.

      1) Similarly, proceeds from a "loss of profits" insurance policy are includable, just as the profits would have been (and the premiums on such a policy are deductible business expenses).

2) If the insurance policy merely provides for a flat per-day benefit during the period the taxpayer is deprived of the use and enjoyment of some business asset, the proceeds are not taxable if the taxpayer uses the total benefits paid to buy or rent similar property.

3. Deferred Payments.

a. **The problem.** In general, I.R.C. section 104(a)(2) excludes the full amount of damages received from personal injury awards. However, a plaintiff will often win a damage award which will be received in monthly payments rather than a lump sum. The issue arising in this context is whether the full amount of the monthly payments is excludable from gross income or only the discounted present value of such payments.

b. **The basic law.** In Rev. Rul. 79-220, 1979-2 C.B. 74, it was held that the full amount of monthly payments received in a damage award was excludable from gross income. In the facts of that case, the taxpayer accepted a damage settlement calling for a lump sum payment of $8,000 and monthly payments of $250 for the taxpayer's lifetime or 20 years (whichever is longer). The taxpayer had no right to control the investment of monies used to fund the monthly amounts. The defendant insurance company purchased a single premium annuity contract to provide for the monthly payments. In that case, the IRS held that the full amount of the $250 monthly payments were excludable from gross income. The Service noted that the taxpayer had no right to receive or control the investment of the monthly payments before they were received by him.

c. **Tax planning.** It is obvious from this Revenue Ruling that a successful plaintiff should structure a damage settlement so that the defendant insurance company would invest a lump sum amount and make periodic payments to him, with no amount of the monies being taxed. The less attractive alternative would be for the taxpayer to receive the lump sum, invest the amount in his own annuity, and be taxed on the income from the investment.

4. Medical Expenses and Other Recoveries.

a. **Introduction.** I.R.C. section 213 provides a limited deduction for amounts paid "for the diagnosis, cure, mitigation, treatment, or prevention of disease, or for the purpose of affecting any structure or function of the body." Medical expenses, including amounts of drugs and insurance premiums, are deductible to the extent they exceed 7.5% of adjusted gross income. [I.R.C. §213(a)]

b. **Medical insurance for employees.** When an employer pays the premium on an employee's medical insurance, the premium is deductible
by the employer but is not included in the employee's income. Also, an
employer-financed plan to reimburse all employees for medical expenses
is not taxable to the employee. Conversely, if an employer pays an
amount to an employee, and the employee invests in his own medical
coverage, the amount paid for coverage is still included in the employee's
gross income.

c. **Other medical expense recoveries.** Section 104(a)(1) excludes work-
ers' compensation from gross income. Likewise, section 105(c) excludes
certain payments from employer insurance for permanent physical injuries.

I. TRANSACTIONS INVOLVING LOANS AND INCOME FROM DISCHARGE OF INDEBTEDNESS

1. **The Basic Rule.** When a debtor obtains forgiveness of a debt absolutely, or
for a payment below the face amount of the debt, the extent of debt forgiven
is income to the debtor. This is true for both nonrecourse loans (where the
lender's security interest is limited to the underlying property) and recourse
loans.

2. **True Discharge of Indebtednes--**

United States v. Kirby Lumber Co., 284 U.S. 1 (1931).

Facts. Kirby (P) issued its own bonds for their face value of $12 million. During the
same year, P repurchased some of the bonds at a discount of $137,521. The IRS claimed
that this was income (as a forgiveness of debt at a lesser amount than the actual debt)
and assessed P accordingly. P paid the tax and brought suit for a refund.

Issue. Does retirement of debt for less than face value represent income to the debtor?

Held. Yes. Judgment for D is affirmed.

♦   Gross income includes "gains or profits" and income derived from any source
whatever. If a corporation sells and then retires bonds at less than their face
value, the excess is gain or income for the taxable year.

---

3. **Exceptions.**

a. **Insolvent debtors.** If a debtor was insolvent both before *and* after the
debt cancellation, the gain realized by the debt cancellation is not in-

come to him. He will recognize income, however, to the extent that the debt cancellation makes the debtor solvent. [I.R.C. §108]

   b.   **Gifts.** If a personal or family relationship is shown, and the debt cancellation was intended as a gift, no income is recognized by the debtor.

   c.   **Contributions to capital.** A shareholder forgiving a debt owed to him by his corporation is looked upon as a contribution to capital and is not income to the corporation.

   d.   **Compromise of disputed claims.** If a cancellation or reduction of debt is in reality a compromise of a disputed claim, rather than a fixed debt, no income is recognized.

4.   **Contested Liability--**

Zarin v. Commissioner, 916 F.2d 110 (3rd Cir. 1990).

Facts. Zarin (P) was a compulsive gambler. During 1978 and 1979, P lost $2,500,000 playing craps at a casino where he had developed a $200,000 line of credit. After the state Casino Control Commissioner issued an order making further extensions of credit to P illegal, the casino continued to extend credit to P. P ran up a debt to the casino in the amount of $3,435,000. The casino filed a court action to collect the debt from P. P claimed that the debt was unenforceable under regulations intended to protect compulsive gamblers. In 1981, the casino and P settled the dispute for $500,000. The Commissioner of Internal Revenue (D) determined a deficiency for P's 1980 return, claiming that P recognized $2,935,000 of income from the discharge of indebtedness (the difference between the $3,435,000 and the $500,000 settlement). The Tax Court held for D. P appeals.

Issue. Does the settlement of a contested liability result in income from discharge of indebtedness?

Held. No. Judgment reversed.

♦   P owed an unenforceable debt to the casino of $3,435,000. After P disputed his obligation to pay the debt, both parties agreed to settle for $500,000. Given the circumstances regarding the enforceability of the debt, both parties agreed that the debt was not worth $3.4 million, but it was worth something. The amount of the debt could not be determined until settlement. Therefore, P was deemed to have owed the casino $500,000, and since he paid the casino $500,000, no income to P was generated.

♦   Additionally, the Code section covering income from discharge of indebtedness [I.R.C. §108] does not apply since P was not liable for the unenforceable debt, and P did not receive property subject to the debt.

---

5. **Amount Realized on Disposition of Encumbered Property.**

   a. **General rule.** When mortgaged property is disposed of, the amount realized not only includes cash received, but also the amount of the mortgage which the taxpayer no longer must pay off. This is true even if the mortgage is nonrecourse in nature (*i.e.*, not subjecting the borrower to personal liability for the loan). In those cases, the mortgagee can only gain satisfaction of the debt from the property itself.

   b. **Gifted property encumbered by gift taxes--**

Diedrich v. Commissioner, 457 U.S. 191 (1982).

Facts. The Diedrichs (Ps) gave 85,000 shares of stock to their three children directly and through a trust. A condition of the gift was that the children would pay all applicable gift taxes. The gift taxes of $62,992 paid by the donees exceeded Ps' basis in the stock ($51,073) by $11,919. A tax deficiency of $5,959 was assessed by the Commissioner (D). The Tax Court held for Ps, but the court of appeals reversed. Ps appeal.

Issue. If a donee pays gift taxes, as a condition of receiving a gift, which exceeds the donor's basis in the gifted property, does the donor realize taxable income?

Held. Yes. Judgment affirmed.

◆   When a gift is made, the gift tax liability falls on the donor. This is as much a legal obligation as a donor's income taxes or a mortgage. When the donee agrees to pay the gift tax, the donor receives an immediate economic benefit of that amount.

◆   Congress has structured gift taxes to encourage transfer. Some exclusion may be forthcoming to exclude conditional gifts or net gifts from income taxation. However, this is a legislative function. The Court is bound by the definition of I.R.C. section 61, which states that gross income is income "from whatever source derived."

Dissent (Rehnquist, J.). In *Old Colony Trust Co. v. Commissioner,* 279 U.S. 716 (1929), it was settled that a taxable transaction had occurred, leaving open the question of the *amount* realized. Here, however, it is unclear that a taxable transaction has in fact taken place. The Court holds the transaction to be taxable by terming the gift a partial sale. Congressional intent is clear that gift transactions are to be subject to a tax system wholly separate from the income tax.

---

6. **Leverage.**

a. **Introduction.** Most properties, while owned by the taxpayer, are financed (or paid for) with borrowed funds. Earnings with a third party's funds is known as leverage. The use of borrowed funds presents the problem of determining the taxpayer's basis for computing gain on disposition or depreciation of the property.

b. **Mortgages and the *Crane* rule--**

Crane v. Commissioner, 331 U.S. 1 (1947).

Facts. Crane (D) inherited an apartment building and land subject to a mortgage. The value of the property equaled the mortgage of $262,000, meaning that D's equity in the real estate was $0. D never assumed the mortgage on the property and in 1938 sold her interest for $3,000. After deducting selling expenses of $500, D claimed a capital gain of $2,500, stating that her adjusted basis in the property was her net equity of $0. In Tax Court, the Commissioner (P) argued that the property acquired and sold was the physical property itself, undiminished by the mortgage. Thus, the IRS position was that the basis was $262,042.50 minus $28,045.10 in allowable depreciation, equaling an adjusted basis of $233,977.40. The amount realized from sale included not only the cash received of $2,500, but also the mortgage subject to which the property was sold. The Tax Court held for D, but the court of appeals reversed. D appeals.

Issue. Is the basis equal to the net value of property less the unassumed mortgage?

Held. No. Judgment affirmed.

♦ A mortgagor, not personally liable on the debt, who sells the property subject to a mortgage and for other consideration, realizes a benefit equal to the amount of the mortgage as well as the additional consideration received.

♦ "Property" is the physical thing which is the subject of ownership, or the sum of the owner's rights to control and dispose of the property.

♦ Depreciation deductions are based on the value of the property. If D's reasoning were used, the depreciation deductions taken on the property would have resulted in a negative basis in the property or be disallowed altogether.

Dissent. D was never personally liable for the debt, and hence was relieved of no debt upon sale of the property.

Comment. The Court stressed the need to include the mortgage in order that the definition of "property" be the same for acquisition, depreciation, and disposition. Had D's basis been zero, she could have taken no depreciation.

---

c.   **Depreciable basis.** The Service allows a taxpayer to claim depreciation on a property value based on the mortgage debt so long as "a bona fide debt obligation" exists. In *Mayerson v. Commissioner,* 47 T.C. 340 (1966), the taxpayer purchased a building and incurred a 99-year mortgage without personal liability and limiting the mortgage's recourse upon default. The Tax Court upheld the taxpayer's inclusion of the debt in his depreciable basis. However, I.R.C. section 465 limits deductions to the amount the taxpayer is "at risk." Consequently, the depreciation deductions in excess of the out-of-pocket costs may not be deductible. In addition, the Tax Reform Act of 1986 added provisions to restrict deductions to the income generated from the property.

d.   **Conclusion.** The *Crane* rule permits a taxpayer to claim depreciation on a basis in excess of his out-of-pocket investment if he purchased the property subject to debt. This is allowed since it is assumed that the taxpayer-mortgagor will make future payments on the debt in order to retain ownership of the property.

e.   **When the mortgage balance exceeds the value of the property sold--**

Commissioner v. Tufts, 461 U.S. 300 (1983).

Facts. A partnership was formed with the purpose of building an apartment complex. Six days later it entered into an agreement with the Farm and Home Savings Association (F & H) for a loan and mortgage of $1,851,500 to finance construction. Under the agreement neither the partnership nor any of the partners (including Tufts (P)) assumed personal liability for repayment of the loan. After the complex was constructed, the partnership had difficulty renting the units, and consequently had difficulty meeting its mortgage payments. Finally, two years after the loan agreement was signed, each partner's interest was sold to a third party (Bayles) for $250 in sales expense and assumption of the mortgage. The property's fair market value at that time was not more than $1,400,000. The Commissioner (D), stating that the partnership had realized the full amount of the nonrecourse obligation, assessed P his share of a $400,000 deficiency. The Tax Court held for D, but the court of appeals reversed. D brings this appeal.

Issue. Does the *Crane* rule regarding nonrecourse mortgages apply where the mortgage exceeds the value of the property disposed of?

Held. Yes. Judgment reversed.

♦   The *Crane* decision requires the amount of a nonrecourse liability to be included in the property's basis and the amount realized on its disposition. This is based on the assumption that the mortgage will be paid in full and represents an obligation to pay.

♦ Absence of personal liability on a mortgage does not relieve the borrower of his obligation to repay, but only limits the mortgagee's remedies on default. When a mortgage is assumed, the borrower is relieved of the obligation to repay monies received tax free.

Concurrence (O'Connor, J.). The logical way to view cases like this is to treat the ownership and sale of property separate from the loan and its retirement. The fair market value would be used as the basis of the property when acquired and sold. As for the assumption of a nonrecourse loan with a value less than the property disposed of, a classic cancellation of indebtedness (with gain recognition) would occur.

Comment. Note that to not require inclusion of the total mortgage assumption in the amount realized would be inconsistent, since a taxpayer includes the amount in computing basis and then claims depreciation on that amount.

---

7. **Borrowing Against Appreciation.** If a taxpayer buys property for $10,000 cash and the property rises in value to $100,000, then the taxpayer has an unrecognized gain of $90,000. Suppose the taxpayer borrows $60,000 on a nonrecourse basis, with the lender's sole security being that of the property. In this case, the taxpayer has "locked in" gain to the extent of $50,000. An argument could be made that the taxpayer has a taxable gain of $50,000 at the time of borrowing the $60,000 (*i.e.*, that gain should be recognized to the extent that loans exceed basis). This is not the case. The taxpayer is not taxed in the year in which the property is encumbered by the loan in excess of basis. When the property is later transferred, the earlier loan proceeds must be treated as proceeds of sale. For example, if the subject property were later transferred for cash of $20,000, with the purchaser assuming debt, the proceeds would equal $80,000 and the gain to be recognized would be $70,000.

J. ILLEGAL INCOME

1. **The Basic Law.** Money or property received due to illegal activities is includable in gross income. This does not amount to tacit approval of the activities, but a recognition that the taxpayer has received economic value or gain which is income. For example, proceeds from prostitution, extortion, embezzlement, and illegal gambling are all taxable income. However, their discovery and collection is a different matter for the IRS.

2. **Illegal Income--**

Gilbert v. Commissioner, 552 F.2d 478 (2d Cir. 1977).

Facts. Gilbert (P) was president, principal stockholder, and a director of the E. L. Bruce Co. In 1961 and 1962, P acquired a substantial personal and beneficial ownership in another company (Celotex), intending to bring a merger of Celotex into Bruce. P persuaded associates to purchase Celotex stock, guaranteeing them against loss. When the stock market later declined, P was called upon to furnish funds for the declining Celotex shares. Lacking cash of his own, P had the secretary of Bruce issue a series of checks totaling $1,958,000 to meet P's obligation. He promptly informed several of Bruce's officers and directors of the withdrawal. Later, P executed interest-bearing promissory notes to secure the monies he owed Bruce. The board refused to ratify Gilbert's unauthorized withdrawals, and when sale of the Celotex stock was rejected, the board demanded P's resignation and issued public notice of his unauthorized withdrawals. P flew to Brazil that night, and the market price of Bruce and Celotex stock both plummeted. The Commissioner (D) filed a tax lien against Gilbert for $1,720,000, claiming that Gilbert received income when he made the unauthorized withdrawals. The Tax Court affirmed, and P appeals.

Issue. Does consensual recognition of an obligation to repay embezzled funds allow that they be treated as a loan rather than income?

Held. Yes. Judgment reversed.

♦ Where a taxpayer withdraws funds from a corporation which he fully intends to repay and which he expects with reasonable certainty that he will be able to repay, where he believes that his withdrawals will be approved by the corporation, and where he makes a prompt assignment of assets sufficient to secure the amount owed, he does not realize income on the withdrawals.

♦ When P acquired the money, there was an express consensual recognition of his obligation to repay by the corporate secretary, officers, directors, and by Gilbert himself.

♦ P's net increase in real wealth on the overall transaction was zero. He had for his own use withdrawn corporate funds but had granted the corporation control over at least an equal amount of his own assets to secure the withdrawal.

Comment. The court made a distinction in this case since the embezzler did not intend at the outset to abscond with the embezzled funds. Thus, an intent to repay embezzled funds carried some weight with this court.

---

3. **Embezzlers.** In *James v. United States*, 366 U.S. 213 (1961), a union official embezzled over $738,000 of funds belonging to a union and an insurance company. The United States Supreme Court held in that case that James should have included the embezzled funds in his gross income, stating that earnings acquired, lawfully or unlawfully, without the consensual recogni-

tion of an obligation to repay and without restriction to their disposition, are income. The dissent in that case cited to the case of *Commissioner v. Wilcox,* 327 U.S. 404 (1946), where it was held that embezzled funds were not income because there was an obligation to restore the funds to the victim. In other words, the embezzler never acquired title to the funds and as such was similar to a borrower of a loan.

K. INTEREST ON STATE AND MUNICIPAL BONDS

1. **Basic Concepts.** I.R.C. section 103 provides that interest on certain obligations of state and local governments is exempt from the federal income tax. This tax break allows governments to borrow money at a reduced rate, since the exclusion of interest will add to the investor's rate of return, particularly those in the higher tax brackets. In effect, this is a subsidy from the federal to the state and local governments. The reason behind this exclusion is to encourage investment in state and municipal bonds. Also, it is constitutionally questionable whether taxing those obligations would be an improper infringement on state and local governments.

2. **Restrictions.** Interest on loans to carry such securities cannot be deducted, and gain realized on the sale of such securities is taxed. Note also that since 1941, the interest on all obligations of the United States and its instrumentalities is fully subject to federal income tax.

3. **Industrial Revenue Bonds.** The rules relating to tax-exempt obligations have been limited by the Tax Reform Acts of 1984 and 1986. As a consequence, there are limitations as to the amount and purpose of industrial revenue bond issues that can be tax exempt. Generally, bonds issued for traditional government activities such as roads, schools, etc., will be available without limit. However, "private activity" bonds will be subject to limitations as to specific uses as well as amounts. Beginning in 1988, the amount of "private activity bonds" will be limited to the greater of $50 per resident or $150 million per state.

4. **United States Treasury Bonds.** The 1988 tax act added I.R.C. section 135, which exempts from taxation the interest earned on certain treasury savings bonds if the proceeds of the bonds do not exceed the tuition and fees incurred for higher education of the taxpayer and/or his dependents. The benefit is phased out as income rises above a certain level.

L. SALE OR EXCHANGE OF A HOME

1. **Primary Residence**. Section 121 excludes some gain on a sale/exchange of a home if the taxpayer has owned the home and used it as a primary residence for periods aggregating two years over a five-year period. Section 121

excludes $250,000 per taxpayer; $500,000 for married taxpayers filing jointly if both have lived in the home for the prescribed time. If a taxpayer does not meet the primary residence requirements due to a change in her place of employment, health, or unforeseen circumstances as provided in the regulations, an exclusion up to a reduced dollar ceiling is permitted.

III. PROBLEMS OF TIMING

A. GAINS FROM INVESTMENT IN PROPERTY

1. Origins.

a. The realization requirement. The most common economic concept of income is the increase of wealth from one point to another, plus what one has consumed in between. So if A buys stock at $20 a share and it is worth $100 a share at the end of the year, there is a gain, and, according to the economic idea, there is "income." However, there is not income for tax purposes. The distinction is founded in the idea of a "realization"; that is, some event must happen to make it appropriate to tax appreciation in value. This event is called a "realization of income."

b. The definition of income--

Eisner v. Macomber, 252 U.S. 189 (1920).

Facts. Macomber (P) received a 50% stock dividend from Standard Oil Co.; *i.e.*, she received an additional share for each two shares that she had previously owned. The Commissioner (D) assessed P with a deficiency, claiming that a stock dividend was income under the Sixteenth Amendment. The court of appeals held for P, and D appeals.

Issue. Is a stock dividend a realization of income?

Held. No. Judgment affirmed.

♦ A stock dividend is a mere transfer of corporate funds from one account to another. The shareholders receive additional stock, but their share in the corporation remains the same.

♦ Income is gain derived from capital, labor, or both. It is not a gain accruing to the capital asset, but something separate and exchangeable. P should not be taxed until she disposes of the stock.

Dissent (Holmes, J.). The common definition of income should embrace this type of transaction.

Dissent (Brandeis, J.). Since P could sell the stock at any time for a cash realization, the receipt of additional stock through a stock dividend should be a taxable event.

Comment. Note also that since *Eisner,* provisions have been placed in the Code for the taxation of stock dividends in certain circumstances (see section 305); for example, where the shareholder has the election of taking stock or cash as the dividend. (One result is that the shareholder, if she takes stock, may end up with a greater proportionate interest than she had before the dividend.)

---

c. **Judicial history.** In *Merchants Loan and Trust Co. v. Smietanka*, 255 U.S. 509 (1921), the Supreme Court stated: "Income may be defined as the gain derived from capital, from labor, or from both combined, *provided it be understood to include profit gained through a sale or conversion of capital assets*." Before this decision, the single isolated sale of property was argued not to produce taxable income. This case put isolated sales on the same footing as sales by those in the business of selling property.

d. **Statutory terminology.** Congress has responded to its power to tax gains from sales of property by gradually producing an ever-increasingly difficult statutory law. The complexity is due primarily to the desire of Congress to give preferential treatment to certain types of assets (*see* VIII, *infra*). The gain or loss from the disposition of property is the difference between the amount realized and the adjusted basis, *infra*. Whether the realized gain or loss is recognized for tax purposes depends on various sections of the Code. In the case of a sale or exchange, sections 1031 to 1039 and other sections of the Code determine whether a realized gain is totally or partially recognized, if at all. These are some of the most complicated sections of the Code.

e. **The realization concept today.** The realization requirement remains as a standard in current tax law. Unrealized gains in property values go untaxed until the point of sale (or realization event). This is partly due to the administrative impossibility (and imprecision) of annually appraising all real property for purposes of taxing gain.

2. **Development: Tenant Improvements--**

Helvering v. Bruun, 309 U.S. 461 (1940).

Facts. In 1915, Bruun (P) leased for 99 years a lot and building which he owned. In 1929, the lessee demolished the building and built a new one on the land. In 1933, the lessee defaulted and P took possession of the land and building. The Commissioner (D) assessed a tax for the difference in value between the new and old buildings. D was overruled in the lower courts and brings this appeal.

Issue. Is a lessor taxable for improvements which a tenant makes on land which is repossessed?

Held. Yes. Judgment reversed.

- It is not necessary to sever the improvement from capital to effect a realization, nor must the asset be sold for cash. This case is different from a stock dividend where the proportional interest remains the same. Here P received a building worth about $50,000 more than the old one.

Comments.

- The court here viewed the repossession as a completed transaction with realizable gain, even though no cash was received by the taxpayer. The *Bruun* result exposed taxpayers to great tax liability in one year. In response to this ruling, Congress enacted I.R.C. section 109, which states that gross income does not include income derived by the lessor of real estate on termination of the lease, representing the value of property attributable to buildings or other improvements made by the lessee. Note, however, that the lessor is liable in the event that the improvements constitute "rent."

- Note that the *Bruun* holding and its statutory progeny do not exempt income from taxation, but merely defer its recognition.

---

3. Nonrecourse Borrowing in Excess of Basis--

Woodsam Associates, Inc. v. Commissioner, 198 F.2d 357 (2d Cir. 1952)

Facts. Mrs. Wood purchased a piece of property in New York City in 1922 for $296,400 that was partly financed by mortgage debt. In 1931, Mrs. Wood refinanced the mortgage, increasing the debt to $400,000. At that time the mortgage became nonrecourse, meaning that she was no longer personally liable to repay the loan, even if the property's value was insufficient to pay off the debt upon default. In 1934, this property was transferred to Woodsam Associates, Inc. (P) in exchange for capital stock. P's tax basis in the property was Mrs. Wood's carryover basis. In 1943, the property was disposed of in a foreclosure sale and P reported gain. P claims that Mrs. Wood should have reported gain in 1934 when she received a loan for which she was not personally liable in an amount greater than her basis in the property. Such gain would have increased P's carryover basis, thereby decreasing the amount of gain recognized upon foreclosure. The Commissioner (D) disallowed the increased basis adjustment and the Tax Court affirmed. P appeals.

Issue. Does the owner's receipt of a nonrecourse loan in an amount greater than her adjusted basis in the mortgage property trigger gain?

Held. No. Judgment affirmed.

- Mrs. Wood never made a disposition of the property to create a taxable event. Each time she borrowed money she retained ownership rights in the property and remained in a position to borrow more money against the property if and when circumstances permitted and she so desired. Realization of gain was postponed until there was a final disposition of the property at the time of the foreclosure sale. Therefore, Mrs. Wood's borrowings did not change the basis for the computation of gain or loss.

---

4. Losses--

Cottage Savings Association v. Commissioner, 499 U.S. 554 (1991).

Facts. Cottage Savings Association (P) is a savings and loan regulated by the Federal Home Loan Bank Board ("FHLBB"). P held many long-term mortgages that had declined in value during the 1970s. P and many other institutions wanted to sell the devalued mortgages to recognize tax-deductible losses, but a corresponding book loss would have put the institutions at risk of closure by the FHLBB. In response to this problem, the FHLBB issued a ruling that allowed institutions to exchange "substantially identical" loan portfolios without recognizing losses for financial purposes. In 1980, P relied upon this ruling and sold "90% participation" in 252 mortgages and simultaneously purchased "90% participation interests" in 305 mortgages. All of the mortgages were secured by single-family homes. The total fair market value of the mortgages sold and purchased was approximately $6.9 million. P claimed a $2,447,091 loss on the disposition of the 252 mortgages on its 1980 tax return. The Commissioner (D) disallowed the deduction and P sought a redetermination in the Tax Court. The Tax Court held for P. The court of appeals reversed, stating that although P's losses were realized, they were not "actually" sustained in 1980 under I.R.C. section 165(a). P appeals.

Issue. Does the exchange of one lender's interests in a group of mortgages for another lender's interests in a different group of mortgages qualify as a taxable disposition of property?

Held. Yes. Judgment reversed.

♦   To realize a gain or loss in the value of property, the taxpayer must engage in a sale or other disposition of property. [I.R.C. §1001] However, an exchange of property gives rise to a realization under section 1001 only if the properties exchanged are "materially different." [Treas. Reg. §1.1001-1] D argues that properties are materially different only if they differ in economic substance, *i.e.*, when the parties, the relevant market, and the relevant regulatory body would consider them material. We reject D's argument and hold that exchanged properties are materially different if they embody legally distinct entitlements. The mortgages P received were made to different obligors and secured by different homes, thus, the exchanged interests did embody legally distinct entitlements. We hold that P realized its losses at the point of the exchange.

♦ The court of appeals disallowed the deduction of P's losses, holding that although P's losses were realized, they were not actually sustained, as required under I.R.C. section 165. We hold that since the transaction was done at arm's length and involved materially different properties, the losses were actually sustained.

Dissent. The FHLBB's ruling lists 10 factors that, when satisfied, serve to classify the interests as substantially identical. In addition to meeting these factors, P retained 10% interests in the loans, and many other facts showed that P was in the same economical situation both before and after the exchange. Income tax law should be concerned with the substance and not the mere form.

---

5.   **Express Nonrecognition Provisions.**

   a.   **Like-kind exchanges.**

      1)   **Introduction.** I.R.C. section 1031(a) states that no gain or loss is recognized on an exchange of business property or property held for investment for receipt of property of a like kind. "Like kind" refers to the general nature of the property, not to its grade, value, or quality. For example, unimproved investment real estate could be exchanged for investment real estate with improvements and still qualify under section 1031(a). The Tax Reform Act of 1986 requires that new property be identified within 45 days of the transaction. In addition, the acquisition of the new property must be completed within 180 days of the transaction.

      2)   **Carryover of basis.** If property is given up for other property in a transaction which qualifies as a like-kind exchange, section 1031(d) requires the taxpayer to use the basis of her traded property as the new basis of her acquired property. This, in effect, allows the taxpayer to postpone any gain recognition until the acquired property is later sold. Thus, section 1031 does not forgive gain recognition, but only postpones it.

      3)   **Effect of "boot."** If a taxpayer receives cash or nonqualifying property (boot) as part of a 1031 exchange, she must recognize her realized gain on the transaction up to the amount of the boot she realized. For example, if a taxpayer exchanges an apartment building with a basis of $60,000 (and a value of $85,000) for an apartment building with a value of $80,000 plus cash of $5,000, her realized gain is $25,000, of which she will have to recognize gain of $5,000 (the amount of the boot).

4) **Qualifying property.** I.R.C. section 1031 does not apply to securities, stock in trade, interest in partnerships or trusts, and choses in action. [*See* I.R.C. §1031(a)(2)] It only applies to property held and used in a trade or business. In Revenue Ruling 82-166, 1982-2 C.B. 190, the IRS ruled that I.R.C. section 1031 does not apply to the exchange of gold bullion for silver bullion.

5) **Nonelective.** Section 1031 is not a provision applicable at the choice of the taxpayer. Thus, when a loss occurs on an exchange of like-kind property, its recognition will be deferred even though the taxpayer would normally desire to claim the loss at the time of the exchange.

b. **Losses from sales of property between related parties.** I.R.C. section 267 disallows deductions for losses from sales of property between related parties. These include transactions between family members, between a corporation and a majority shareholder, and others. However, even though the seller is unable to claim a loss, the purchaser of the property is allowed to reduce any gain to the extent the loss was previously disallowed. [I.R.C. §267(d)]

1) **Example.** If A sells a tractor having a basis of $12,000 to his son B for $10,000, A cannot deduct the loss. However, when B later sells the tractor to a third party for $15,000, B will be allowed to use A's loss ($2,000) in computing his gain. B's gain in this case would be $3,000 instead of $5,000.

c. **Involuntary conversions.**

1) **Introduction.** Section 1033 governs the taxability of a receipt of insurance proceeds or an eminent domain award from the involuntary conversion of a taxpayer's property. This section states that no gain shall be recognized on the conversion of property into similar property. In addition, no gain shall be recognized on the conversion of property into money, provided that property "similar or related in use" is purchased within a two-year period after the conversion. However, gain will be taxed to the extent that the proceeds from the conversion exceed the taxpayer's replacement cost. The basis of the new property is equal to the basis of the converted property plus any gain recognized.

d. **Sale or exchange of the taxpayer's residence.** Section 1034 allows a taxpayer to not recognize the gain on the sale of his home if he purchases (or completes constructing) a new residence within two years of the sale. Gain is recognized, however, to the extent that the proceeds of the sale of the old residence exceed the cost of the new one. The basis of the new residence is reduced by the amount of gain not recognized on the sale of the old residence. Also, section 121 allows a taxpayer of 55 or older to exclude from tax the gain attributable to the first $125,000 of the price of the sale of his residence, provided that the house was owned and used as his principal residence for at least three of the last five years prior to its sale.

e. **Wash sales.** When a taxpayer sells stock or securities and within 30 days before or after the sale buys substantially identical assets, such a transaction is called a wash sale. Section 1091 provides that losses from wash sales are not deductible. The new securities retain the basis of the old securities, adjusted for the difference between the selling price of the old securities and the purchase price of the new securities. Note, however, that section 1091 applies only to wash sale losses. A taxpayer is still permitted to claim gain on wash sales. This could be done if a taxpayer wishes to step up his basis in his stock or securities, and has capital losses against which the wash sale gains can be offset.

6. **Corporate Reorganizations and Transfers to Controlled Corporations.** If the shareholders of corporation A exchange their stock for stock in corporation B, the exchange does not fall under I.R.C section 1031 because securities are excluded from its coverage. However, the exchange would generally qualify as a nontaxable event under the corporate reorganization provision of I.R.C. sections 354 and 367(a)(1). Their review is extremely complex and beyond the scope of this text.

B. ORIGINAL ISSUE DISCOUNT AND I.R.C. SECTION 483

The Original Issue Discount (O.I.D.) rules are contained in I.R.C. sections 1272 to 1275. The intent of these sections is to insure that transactions reflect the time value of money. For example, if a transaction involving the sale of property does not reflect a market interest rate, such a rate will be imputed. These rules are applied to both cash and accrual basis taxpayers. The O.I.D. rules apply to the issuance of debt instruments as well as the sale of property.

1. **I.R.C. Section 483.** This section requires that the unstated interest element in contracts for the sale of property with deferred payments be treated as interest. The result of this is that part of the seller's amount realized on the sale of property must be reduced for the interest element of the obligation. This in effect separates the cost of the property from the cost of allowing future payments of the debt. For example: A sells to B land worth $60,000 for $20,000 down and two yearly payments of $20,000. A does not charge B interest on the $40,000 of deferred payments. The Code requires that a part of the amount A realized on the sale of the land be counted as interest. The section specifies the method for computing how much of the two yearly payments is interest. I.R.C. section 483 covers only transactions not subject to the O.I.D. rules.

C. OPEN TRANSACTIONS, INSTALLMENT SALES, AND DEFERRED SALES

1. Open Transactions.

a. **The "open transaction" doctrine.** The amount of gain or loss is determined by the difference between the "amount realized" on a disposition and the "*adjusted basis*" of the property relinquished. If the amount realized is unknown or uncertain, the gain or loss cannot be measured and the transaction is an "open transaction." The regulations under I.R.C. section 1001 state that open transactions occur in only rare and extraordinary circumstances. It is the IRS's position that the fair market value of the amount realized can always be determined or reasonably estimated.

b. **Timing and character of gain--**

Burnet v. Logan, 283 U.S. 404 (1931).

Facts. Logan (P) and others sold their stock in an iron company that owned an interest in an iron ore mine. In return, P received cash plus an agreement that the buyer of the stock would pay P 60¢ for each ton of ore extracted from the mine. The Commissioner (D) ruled that each payment for extracted ore could be allocated between the return of capital and taxable gain. D argued that the value of the future payments for the ore could be reasonably estimated. The court of appeals, however, ruled that it was impossible to determine the fair market value of the agreement. Therefore, P could allocate all payments thereunder to return of capital before recognizing any gain. D appeals.

Issue. In an open-ended transaction where the amount to be received is not determinable, can the seller recover his basis before recognizing any tax liability?

Held. Yes. Judgment affirmed.

♦ The transaction was not a closed one. The consideration for the sale was $2,200,000 in cash and the promise of future money payments that were contingent upon facts and circumstances not possible to foretell with any fair certainty. The promise was in no proper sense equivalent to cash and had no ascertainable fair market value.

Comment. All payments received under the "open transaction" approach of *Burnet v. Logan* are taxed as *capital gains,* after basis has been recovered. But if the contract can be valued, and the transaction closed, an immediate gain or loss is computed. Moreover, if the taxpayer later recovers more than the value of the contract, the profit is *ordinary income.*

c. **Consequences of characterization.** If a transaction is treated as closed, the seller may lose the benefit of capital gains treatment. In *Waring v. Commissioner*, 412 F.2d 800 (3rd Cir. 1969), P sold a license to use his name for a right to receive royalties. An accountant valued the right at $300,000. For the first few years after the sale, the royalties were treated as recovery of capital reducing the basis. After receiving $300,000 in royalties, the royalties became ordinary income. P realized that he should have characterized the sale as an open transaction. P claimed this error and filed subsequent tax returns to reflect capital gains treatment of the royalties. However, the court denied P's claim in light of the accountant's ability to easily characterize the value of the royalty right at $300,000 when the license was first sold.

    1) **Comment.** In a closed transaction, all royalty payments in excess of basis are considered as part of the original royalty contract, and are therefore ordinary income. In an open transaction, the subsequent payments are deemed to be additional return on the sale or exchange which produced the capital gain (in this case the stock for assets exchange).

d. **Annuities.**

    1) **Definition.** An annuity is an investment which is paid back, with interest, for a set period of time or for life. The part of each payment which is a return of the taxpayer's investment is not taxed. The interest portion, however, is taxable. [See I.R.C. §72] For example, A pays $5,000 now, which entitles him to $100 a month for life beginning when he reaches 65 years of age. This is an annuity.

    2) **Treatment.** Calculating the nontaxable return of capital portion is done by determining the exclusion ratio. I.R.C. section 72(b) defines the exclusion ratio as the cost of the annuity divided by the expected return. The expected return is calculated by either a fixed contract or by reference to the life expectancy of the investor. This is determined from actuarial tables (for example, in the case above, the taxpayer's life expectancy at age 65 would be seven years). The amount excluded from each payment is the product of the exclusion ratio and the payment. The amount of each payment which exceeds this return of capital portion is then taxed as net income. Note that certain employee pension plans that work quite similarly to annuities are treated differently.

e. **The effect of the method of accounting on the amount realized.** It has been litigated whether the certainty of determination of fair market value of property received is affected by the taxpayer's method of accounting. When merchandise is sold to customers for receivables such as notes, checks, or open accounts, the inclusion in income depends on the taxpayer's accounting method. Under the accrual method, the receivable represents an unconditional right to payment, and therefore is includable in income. Under the cash method, the receivable is property and is includable as income when received if it is the "equivalent of cash."

2. **Installment Sales.** Section 453 allows taxpayers to elect to defer income taxes until payments are received. It can be elected only for sales of property in installments. The installment method is directed to the problem of having to recognize the gain in the year of sale, even when the cash from the sale has not been received. Under the installment method, the profit is prorated over the term of the payments. To compute the gain, which is recognizable each year, first a fraction of "gross profit" over the "total" contract price is computed. This fraction is applied to each future installment payment made to determine how much of the installment is gain to the seller. The Tax Reform Act of 1986 modified the installment sale rules. The installment method has been eliminated for sales of publicly traded stocks and securities and sales using revolving credit plans. The new rules modify other installment sales by treating a portion of the seller's outstanding debt obligations as an amount received on the installment contract.

D. CONSTRUCTIVE RECEIPT

1. **The Problem.** For a cash basis taxpayer, income is recognized when it is "received" and deductions are taken when "paid." A cash basis taxpayer may in some cases materially affect his net income by accelerating or postponing receipt of income or payment of expenses.

2. **The Doctrine.** Treas. Reg. section 1.446-1(c) states that generally, under the cash receipts and disbursements method in the computation of taxable income, all items that constitute gross income (whether in the form of cash, property, or services) are to be included for the taxable year in which they are actually or constructively received. Sometimes, however, the property that the cash basis taxpayer receives is a claim against another in the form of a check, note, or account receivable. If these are to be includable income when received, then the difference between the cash and accrual methods of tax accounting would be largely eliminated. The courts have therefore constrained the literal language of the regulations and have reduced the required income inclusion of the cash basis taxpayer to cash and cash equivalents. Therefore, an item may be income even though paid in a medium other than cash. For example, a salary payment in the form of property is income to the extent of the fair market value of the property.

3. Limitation--

Amend v. Commissioner, 13 T.C. 178 (1949).

Facts. Amend (P) sold wheat to Burrus in 1944. The wheat was shipped in August, but it was agreed that payment was not to be made until January of 1945. Burrus paid for the wheat by check in January of 1945, but the Commissioner (D) asserted that the amount should be included in P's gross income of 1944. P brings this suit.

Issue. Does a cash basis taxpayer constructively receive income when he receives a promise to pay in the future?

Held. No. Judgment for P.

◆ The basis of the constructive receipt doctrine is that, for tax purposes, income is realized when it is made subject to the will and control of the taxpayer and can be, except for his own action or inaction, reduced to actual possession. Such is not the case here, since P had no legal right to demand and receive his cash from the 1944 sale until 1945 under the terms of the contract.

4. **The Claim of Right Doctrine.** Under the claim of right doctrine, if a taxpayer receives money or property, claims he is entitled to it, and can freely dispose of or consume it, the income from such receipt is immediately taxable. The doctrine applies whether the taxpayer is on a cash or accrual basis.

5. **Deferred Compensation Plans.** These plans involve an employer providing compensation to employees in years after the employees' services are performed. Unless the plan is carefully structured, the entire employee benefit will be taxed in the year earned (not when paid) under the constructive receipt doctrine or as an equivalent of cash. Before services are rendered, the employer and employee should settle the terms of the deferral. Congress has legislated certain types of plans that, if followed, will defer income to the employee until it is actually paid.

6. **Constructive Payment and the Equivalence of Cash.** There is no reference in the Code to constructive expenditures. Thus, there is no constructive payment doctrine as a companion to the constructive receipt doctrine. The reason for this unsymmetrical treatment is that deductions are a matter of legislative grace and are to be strictly construed. Therefore, a deduction cannot be claimed until the year in which it is actually paid out with cash or by some other legal method.

7. **Constructive Receipt and the Economic Benefit Doctrine--**

Pulsifer v. Commissioner, 64 T.C. 245 (1975).

Facts. Gordon Pulsifer acquired an Irish Hospital Sweepstakes ticket in his name and the names of his three children (Ps). Their ticket was represented by a horse named Saratoga Skiddy that placed second in the Lincolnshire Handicap, earning Pulsifer and the children $48,000. Under Irish law, the portion of the winnings payable to Ps could not be released but was put into an interest-bearing account. The money could then be released when Ps reached 21 or application was made by an appropriate guardian on their behalf. The Commissioner (D) assessed a deficiency against Ps, stating that they should be taxed in 1969, when the horse won on their behalf. Ps brought this case to the Tax Court.

Issue. Does the economic benefit doctrine apply, so that Ps are taxed on income prior to its actual receipt?

Held. Yes. Judgment for D.

♦ Ps are mistaken in their contention that all they held in 1969 was a nonassignable chose in action. Under the economic benefit theory, a cash basis taxpayer is taxed on the absolute right to income in the form of a fund which is irrevocably set aside in trust and beyond the reach of creditors.

♦ In this case Ps had an absolute right to their winnings held on deposit. All that was required to receive the money was for their legal representative to apply for it, which he in fact did.

E. DEFERRED COMPENSATION

1. Taxability of Deferred Compensation--

Minor v. United States, 772 F.2d 1472 (9th Cir. 1985).

Facts. Minor (P) was a physician under contract with Snohomish County Physicians Corporation ("Snohomish"). Snohomish adopted a "Supplemental Deferred Compensation Agreement." The agreement allowed Minor to elect to defer between 10% and 90% of his compensation. Minor elected to defer 50% of his compensation through November 30, 1970, and 90% thereafter. The deferred funds were held in trust. The trustee purchased annuity contracts that were payable to beneficiaries upon retirement, death, or disability. The Commissioner (D) assessed P with deficiencies, claiming that the deferred income should be taxed currently. The Tax Court held for P, and D appeals.

Issue. Is deferred compensation put in trust constructively received by the taxpayer and therefore taxed currently?

Held. No. Judgment affirmed.

Comment. To defer compensation, the courts have held that the taxpayer must not receive current economic benefit. Consequently, the deferred compensation plans must be "unfunded." Plans have been held to be unfunded where the trusts holding the funds are subject to the employer's creditors' claims.

---

2. **Qualified Plans.**

   a. **Introduction.** If an annuity or single payment is part of a qualified pension or profit sharing plan, no tax is payable in the year in which the employer contributes to the plan. The tax is deferred until the employee receives payment. This usually occurs after the employee retires and is in a lower tax bracket.

   b. **Types.**

      1) **Defined benefits plans.** In this type of plan, employer payments are made on an actuarial basis designed to provide a specific benefit, usually commencing upon retirement. The employer receives a deduction when amounts are contributed to qualified plans. The benefit formula used is often based on years of service and level of compensation.

      2) **Defined contribution plans.** These plans pay into the employee's account a specific sum. A common defined contribution plan is called a "profit sharing" plan. Under these plans, employers pay a percentage of the company profits into the employee's account. These plans may or may not provide adequately for the employee upon retirement because they are funded only if the company has sufficient profits available each year to fund the employee's account.

   c. **Qualifications.** For a pension or profit sharing plan to receive favorable tax treatment, it must meet statutory requirements set out in I.R.C. section 401. They are very complicated and subject to extensive interpretation. The principal requirements for qualification are set out below.

      1) **Nondiscrimination.** To qualify, a plan must not discriminate on its face or in application in favor of officers, shareholders, or key employees. [I.R.C. §401(a)(4)]

2) **Participation.** Generally, employees must be eligible to participate in a plan at the later of (i) one year of service or (ii) upon reaching 21 years of age. [I.R.C. §410(a)(1)(A)]

3) **Vesting.** I.R.C. section 411 provides that benefits under a plan will be lost if an employee's service is terminated soon after it begins. While the section offers alternatives, the simplest provides that all employer-paid benefits must fully vest after 10 years of service. Plans which provide a large portion of the benefits to highly compensated employees are required to vest participants under accelerated vesting schedules. Employee contributions must be fully vested immediately.

3. **Nonqualified, Unfunded Plans.** Employer contributions to a nonqualified employees' trust or annuity plan are taxed to the employee when his rights first become transferable or nonforfeitable. The amount subject to tax is the value of the employee's interest in the trust or annuity at the time it becomes taxable. Of course, any subsequent employee contributions are taxable to the employee when made. Employers receive a deduction for contributions to these plans when the amounts become taxable to the employee. [*See* I.R.C. §§83, 402(b), 403(c), 404, 405(a)(5)]

4. **Individual Retirement Accounts.** Another commonly used qualified plan is an "individual retirement account" (IRA), which is available to an employed person who is not covered by any other qualified pension or profit sharing plan, or is covered by another qualified plan and has income under a certain amount. Taxpayers with income in excess of these amounts can make contributions to IRAs. However, they cannot claim a deduction for such contributions.

5. **Stock Options.**

   a. **Historical status of stock options.**

      1) **Qualified stock option plans.** Prior to the Tax Reform Act of 1976, qualified stock option plans were allowed (under I.R.C. sections 421-422), so that no tax was assessed at the time the options were given *or* when they were exercised, but the return was taxed at capital gains rates when the stock was sold. The plan had to meet the following requirements:

         a) The option price could not be less than the fair market value of the stock at the time the option was granted;

         b) The taxpayer could not dispose of the stock for three years after exercise;

c) The taxpayer must have been an employee of the employer within three months of the exercise;

d) Options were not exercisable for more than five years from the time granted; and

e) The options had to be nontransferable.

b. **Incentive stock option requirements.**

1) **Incentive stock options.** The qualified stock option, which was repealed in 1976, returned under the new name of "incentive stock option." Under this ERTA provision, a corporate employer can grant an employee an option to purchase its stock; the employer is not taxed when the option is granted nor when it is exercised. The employee is simply taxed (as capital gain or loss) when the stock is ultimately sold. The employer gets no deduction at any time. (Contrast the nonqualified stock option: The employee is almost always taxed for ordinary income on the difference between the value of the stock and the option price when he or she exercises the option, and the employer gets a compensating deduction at the same time.)

2) **Example.** There are very detailed requirements for incentive stock options. For example, the employee may not dispose of the stock for a period extending two years after the option was granted and one year after exercising it (these requirements are waived if the employee dies). In addition, the option price must equal or exceed the value of the stock when the option is granted, the term of the option cannot exceed 10 years, it must be nontransferable, and the employee cannot own more than 10% of the stock (a requirement waived if the option price is at least 110% of the value of the stock when it is granted). Not more than $100,000 per year of stock plus a "carryover amount" can be made subject to stock options. The "carryover amount" is one-half of the amount by which $100,000 exceeded the amount of stock subject to options in any of the past three years.

c. **Nonqualified stock options.** Nonqualified stock options have not been given the same favorable tax treatment as qualified options. The question is always how much of the gain made as a result of receiving an option is to be taxed as ordinary income.

1) If the option has a "readily ascertainable fair market value," then the grant of the option is a taxable event (permitting subsequent appreciation to be taxed at capital gains rates).

2) If not, then on exercise of the option (assuming the underlying shares are not subject to some kind of restriction), the difference between the option price and the fair market value of the stock acquired is taxable at ordinary income rates.

3) Prior to the 1969 Tax Reform Act, it was possible to place certain types of restrictions on the underlying shares (making them non-transferable, etc.) and the taxpayer earned favorable tax treatment; *i.e.*, he received present ownership, deferment of tax until a future year (when restrictions lapsed or the stock was sold), and tax on the growth in value from the time of receipt of the stock to be taxed at capital gains rates. However, I.R.C. section 83, added in 1969, has largely denied these tax benefits to restricted property.

d. Restricted property.

1) **Introduction.** In a restricted stock plan, an employer transfers stock to employees where the stock is subject to some restrictions that affect its value. Prior to 1969, no tax was imposed until the restrictions on the stock lapsed.

2) **Present law.** If the stock is not subject to a substantial risk of forfeiture, the recipient must include in income the excess of the fair market value of the restricted property (such as stock) over what was paid for it. A substantial risk of forfeiture exists where the person's rights to full enjoyment of the property are conditioned upon his future performance of substantial services.

e. Employee stock ownership plans.

1) **Introduction.** An employee stock ownership plan (ESOP) is a qualified deferred compensation plan whereby the plan trustee borrows funds to purchase stock of the employer corporation. The employer then makes deductible contributions to the trust to pay off the loan.

f. Readily ascertainable fair market value--

Cramer v. Commissioner, 64 F.3d 1406 (9th Cir. 1995).

Facts. Cramer, Boynton, and Monaghan (Ps) were employees of IMED, a non-publicly traded corporation. Each of these three individuals received IMED stock options that vested over a five-year period. The stock options contained various transfer restrictions. Ps received informal advice that it may be possible to make section 83(b) elections to cover the options. Under an 83(b) election, they include the value of the options as ordinary income at the time of grant, even if they were not publicly traded, and then the options would receive capital gains treatment upon later disposition. As part of this advice, Ps were also made aware that Treasury Regulations would not allow Ps to make an 83(b) election since the value of the options could not be readily ascertained. Section 83(b) elections were attached to the taxpayers' returns for most of the options for the year of receipt. The filed elections stated that the value of the options was zero at the time of grant. Ps knew at the time of making the election that the options must have had some value. In 1982, IMED was acquired and all outstanding options were purchased. Cramer received $25,945,506, Boynton received $7,714,800, and Monaghan received $2,274,895 for the options. Tax professionals prepared all of Ps' 1982 tax returns. Ps were told that they had a plausible position that the gain from sale of options was capital gain, but they were explicitly told that Treasury Regulations were to the contrary. No disclosure was made on the returns to reflect that positions were taken contrary to the regulations, or to reflect that section 83(b) elections had been made. In fact, it appears that misrepresentations were made on the returns designed to avoid audit. Upon audit, the IRS determined that the sale of options generated ordinary income and calculated deficiencies accordingly. The IRS also assessed penalties for intentional disregard of tax rules and for substantial understatement of tax. The Tax Court upheld both the deficiency and the penalties. Ps appeal.

Issue. Do non-publicly traded stock options have a readily ascertainable fair market value at date of grant?

Held. No.

♦ The Treasury Regulations regarding this issue are reasonable. Based on the regulations, the IMED options clearly failed to meet all of the conditions necessary to make a valid section 83(b) election. Therefore, all of the gain at the time of sale was ordinary.

♦ We also uphold the penalties. Ps had clearly taken a position that they knew was contrary to the Treasury Regulations without making any of the appropriate disclosures. The fact that Ps had also made attempts to bury the option issue in their returns reflected negatively on Ps' case.

F. TRANSFERS INCIDENT TO A DIVORCE OR SEPARATION AGREEMENT

1. Gain Recognized by Transferor--

United States v. Davis, 370 U.S. 65 (1962).

Facts. Davis (P) transferred 1,000 shares of stock to his wife prior to their divorce. This was in settlement of all of the wife's inchoate rights to P's property, including dower and intestate succession. These rights gave her no right to any of the property until P died. The Commissioner (D) held the settlement to be a taxable transfer, and assessed P with a deficiency. P argued that the settlement was not a transfer but a mere division of property owned by the two spouses. The Court of Claims held for P, and D appeals.

Issue. Is a property settlement pursuant to divorce a taxable event?

Held. Yes. Judgment reversed.

♦ The inchoate property rights which a wife possesses under Delaware law do not even remotely reach the dignity of co-ownership. She must survive P to share in his estate. Since the wife was not a co-owner in the property, it must be concluded that a transfer of ownership occurred.

♦ The Court of Claims held that no transaction occurred since the value of the property received by P (*i.e.*, the wife's inchoate marital rights) could not be determined. This is not the case. Assuming that the transaction was made at arm's length, the value of the properties exchanged is presumed to be equal. Therefore, P's amount realized is equal to the fair market value of the stock which he transferred to his wife. P should be taxed on this amount, less the adjusted basis of the stock.

Comment. The *Davis* case has produced variations in the way settlements in common law states and community property states must be taxed. In a community property state, each spouse owns a share of the property. In such a state, the *Davis* settlement would clearly have been a division of co-owned property. The Tax Reform Acts of 1984 and 1986 changed the rules related to divorce settlements. I.R.C. section 1041 states that "no gain or loss shall be recognized on a transfer of property from an individual to a spouse or former spouse, but only if the transfer is incident to the divorce." Consequently, the *Davis* case is not applicable to divorce cases after July 18, 1984.

---

2. **Prenuptial Settlements--**

Farid-Es-Sultaneh v. Commissioner, 160 F.2d 812 (2d Cir. 1947).

Facts. Taxpayer (P) and her future husband entered into a prenuptial agreement whereby she was to receive shares of stock in his company in return for her relinquishment of her rights to support and any inchoate interest in his property. His cost basis in the stock was 16¢ per share. This would be P's basis if it is determined that she received the stock by gift. The stock had a value of $10.67 at the date of her acquisition. This would be the basis of the stock if her acquisition was not by way of gift, but for consideration. P sold the stock in 1938 and used the higher (fair market) value as her basis in computing gain. This had the effect of reducing the gain. The Commissioner (D), determining the acquisition to be a gift, assessed a deficiency and P appealed. The Tax Court held for the Commissioner and P appeals.

Issue. Did P receive the stock as a gift?

Held. No. Judgment reversed.

♦ No absolute gift was made since the transfer was contingent upon the death of P's fiance before the marriage.

Dissent. The majority's characterization of the transaction as being a sale is clearly erroneous. The transfer was to protect P from property loss if her fiance were to die prior to their marriage. This was a gift made with the motive of stimulating marriage.

Comment. Had P lost, the basis of her stock would be the donor's basis (16¢ per share). Since it was held not to be a gift, the basis is the value of the stock at the date of transfer (its market value). In the gift situation, for computing gain, the donee takes the donor's basis. For computing loss, the donee's basis is the fair market value at the date of the gift or the donor's basis, whichever is lower.

---

3. **Alimony, Child Support, and Property Settlements.**

   a. **Alimony vs. child support.** Only payments in cash made for the spouse's maintenance and support are tax deductible. Payments for the support of minor children are not deductible. Care must be taken that payments are specifically characterized as one or the other. To be deductible as alimony, the following conditions must be met:

      1) The payment must be in cash.

      2) The payment must be paid under an "instrument" of divorce.

      3) The parties must not have agreed that the payments are nondeductible.

      4) The parties must not live in the same household.

      5) The payment cannot continue after the death of the payee spouse.

      6) The payments must not be child support.

   b. **Excess front loading.** Taxpayers are required to include in income "excess" alimony amounts paid during the first two years after the divorce. The "excess" amounts are determined as follows:

Year 1 payments minus (average of year 2 and 3 payments + $15,000)

Plus

Year 2 payments minus (year 3 payments + $15,000)

The excess amount is included in income in year 3.

    c.   **Property settlements.** Unlike alimony, payments made as a division of jointly held or community property are not income to the recipient since such payment merely constitutes a liquidation of property already owned by the spouse.

    d.   **Defaulting on child support--**

Diez-Arguelles v. Commissioner, 48 T.C.M. 496 (1984).

Facts. Christina Diez-Arguelles (P) divorced her husband, Kevin Baxter, in 1972. Pursuant to the divorce settlement, Baxter was supposed to pay $300/month for child support. By 1978, he was in arrears in the amount of $4,325. In 1979, he owed $3,000 more in child support. The lack of child support forced P and her new husband to bear all the support for P's two children from her first marriage. The support they paid far exceeded the amounts P's ex-husband owed. P deducted $4,325 as a nonbusiness bad debt from 1978 gross income as a short-term capital gain loss. On her 1979 return, P deducted the $3,000 using the same method. The Commissioner disallowed both deductions. P appeals.

Issue. May a spouse who does not receive child support payments from the former spouse characterize the amounts owed as nonbusiness bad debts and deduct them as a short-term capital loss?

Held. No. Judgment affirmed.

    ♦   An ordinary taxpayer may only deduct nonbusiness bad debts as a capital loss when such debts become completely worthless. Such debts are only deductible to the extent of the taxpayer's basis in the debts.

    ♦   P argues that the basis in the debt is the amount she expended from her income to support her children in excess of the amount that her former spouse paid. However, prior cases have held in effect that the taxpayer had no basis in delinquent support payments. The cases state that an uncollectible support obligation of a former spouse to pay a fixed amount for support was not a bad debt, because the taxpayer was not out of pocket anything due to the former spouse's failure to pay.

---

4. **Division of Property by Unrelated Co-owners.**

   a. **Introduction.** The question of whether a division of property interests or the conversion of property interests to a different form creates a recognition transaction arises not only between spouses but also between unrelated parties.

   b. **Stock and securities.** In Rev. Rul. 56-437, 1956-2 C.B.507, it was held that a conversion of a joint tenancy of corporate stock to a tenancy in common was a nontaxable transaction. Also, the severance of a joint tenancy in stock into two separate ownerships of one-half of the total amount was a nontaxable transaction.

   c. **Real property.** In Rev. Rul. 79-44, 1979-1 C.B. 265, two individuals each owned undivided one-half interests in two parcels of land which they farmed. It was arranged whereby the two parties each ended up owning 100% of one parcel each. The two parcels had the same fair market value and basis. However, one parcel was subject to a mortgage. Therefore, the party receiving the encumbered property also received a note from the other party in the amount of one-half the mortgage. It was held in that case that the transaction was an exchange under section 1001(a)(2). However, it was also held that section 1031 applied since the properties were of a like kind. This meant that gain was deferred on the transaction.

G. AVERAGING

There are situations when strict application of the annual accounting period concept would produce undue hardship. When money received in one year must be repaid in a later year, or when income earned over a number of years is received in one year, the annual accounting period concept should be relaxed.

1. **Income Averaging.** The Tax Reform Act of 1986 repealed income averaging. Prior to 1987, sections 1301-1305 of the Code provided a way for taxpayers with fluctuating yearly incomes to average out the high income so that it was taxed as if received over several years.

2. **Loss Carryovers.** The possibility that a taxpayer will be able to utilize the "tax benefit" rule is greatly reduced by section 172 of the Code. This provision permits a net operating loss to be carried back three years and then carried forward 15 years to offset the income in these years. Even though the loss will not bring a tax benefit in the year of loss, it will do so as it is carried back and forward.

   a. **Net operating loss calculation.** If an individual taxpayer's business deductions (expenses, depreciation, bad debts, etc.) exceed his income, he has a net operating loss. Only expenditures attributable to a taxpayer's trade or business are included in this calculation. Personal deductions and investment deductions are not part of a net operating loss.

H. THE ACCRUAL METHOD AND PREPAID INCOME

1. **Introduction.** The question of when income is taxed depends on two factors. The first is the taxpayer's method of accounting. Section 446 provides that taxpayers shall compute taxable income "under the method of accounting on the basis of which the taxpayer regularly computes his income in keeping his books." However, the method must "clearly reflect income."

2. **Definition of Accrual Accounting.** This method of accounting recognizes items of income when they are *earned*, regardless of when they are received. Also, expense items are recognized when they are *incurred*, regardless of when they are actually paid. Problems of applying the accrual method usually arise in two contexts: (i) where it is uncertain whether an amount will be paid, and (ii) where an amount is received before it has been earned. The Tax Reform Act of 1986 requires corporate and certain other taxpayers with annual gross receipts in excess of $5 million to use the accrual method of accounting.

3. **The Accrual Concept--**

Georgia School-Book Depository v. Commissioner, 1 T.C. 463 (1943).

Facts. Georgia School-Book Depository (D) represented school book publishers in book sales to the State of Georgia. It was paid a percentage commission by the publishers when sales were made, and used the accrual method of accounting. During the taxable years in question, the state fund was not large enough to pay for the books it purchased. The Commissioner (P), however, asserted that D should still claim the income when the books were sold. D brings this suit.

Issue. Should D accrue its commissions when the books are sold by the publisher?

Held. Yes. Judgment for P.

♦ It is the right to receive money which justifies its inclusion in income to an accrual basis taxpayer. Here, D has done everything that was required to claim a right to the income, except receive the proceeds and turn them over to the publishers. If a contingency makes the ultimate receipt of income doubtful, it need not be included as income until received. However, in this case there was very little doubt that the state would ultimately pay.

Comment. The crucial event for accrual basis taxpayers is when payment is actually made. Treas. Reg. section 1.451-1(a) states that "under an accrual method of accounting, income is includable when all the events have occurred which fix the right to receive such income and the amount thereof can be determined with reasonable accuracy." In this regard, the income is includable in the year in which it is earned, regardless of what year the income is actually received.

---

4.   **Prepaid Income--**

American Automobile Association v. United States, 367 U.S. 687 (1961).

Facts. American (P) was an accrual basis taxpayer that prorated membership fees received during the year to cover the months that the fees were meant to cover. P then recognized income only for the prorated amount that fell within the taxable year. The Commissioner (D) contends that P should recognize as income the entire amount of dues received during the taxable year. The Court of Claims held for D, and P appeals.

Issue. Should advance dues paid by club members be included in gross income of the club for the year received?

Held. Yes. Judgment affirmed.

♦   Congress has authorized the accounting method employed by P only in instances of prepaid subscription income, and has specifically refused such authorization for automobile associations. Since Congress has not authorized such an accounting method, the Court should defer to the Commissioner's discretion in denying it.

Dissent (Stewart, Douglas, Harlan, Whittaker, JJ.). The effect of this decision is to disallow a taxpayer from using a generally accepted accounting method and forcing it to use a hybrid method by employing a cash basis for dues received.

Comment. Under generally accepted accounting principles, income is not recognized until it is earned by delivery of the goods or services that the income is paying for. However, the IRS has taken the position that such amounts are income when they are received (independent of when delivery of the goods sold is made). But Rev. Proc. 71-21, 1971-2 C.B. 549, permits the taxpayer in certain instances to defer recognition of income until it is earned. The ruling applies only to a taxpayer who receives prepayment for future delivery of services. Deferment is allowed only if the services are to be rendered in full by the end of the tax year succeeding the tax year of prepayment. The ruling sets out guidelines and examples which illustrate the concept. Supreme Court cases have held that prepaid income is taxable when received. However, one lower court ruling, *Artnell Co. v. Commissioner,* 400 F.2d 981 (7th Cir. 1968), held that a taxpayer will be permitted deferment if he can show that such would be the only proper way to account for the income. *Artnell* involved receipts by the Chicago White Sox baseball team in one taxable year for tickets, parking, and television rights for games to be played in the following taxable year.

---

5. Cash Advances--

Westpac Pacific Food v. Commissioner, 457 F.3d 970 (9th Cir. 2006).

Facts. Westpac (P), a partnership formed by three grocery store chains to purchase and warehouse inventory, signed four contracts, each specifying a quantity of inventory to be purchased. Each contract also provided P a cash advance and a repayment obligation on a pro rata basis if the partnership failed to purchase the quantity specified. P accounted for the cash advances as liabilities, and it reduced the cost of goods sold by a percentage of the advance as goods were purchased. The government reclassified the advances as income when received. The Tax Court agreed with the Commissioner (D) and held that P should have reported the cash advances as income. P appeals.

Issue. Is a discount in the form of a cash advance income when received?

Held. No. Judgment reversed.

♦ D argues that the cash advances were gross income because P had complete dominion over the money; P could spend the money as it chose. However, one may have complete dominion over money, but it does not become income until it is an "accession to wealth." Borrowed money is not income, even though the borrower has complete dominion over it; the loan proceeds do not qualify as income to the taxpayer because of his repayment obligation. In this case, the cash advances were not an accession to wealth, because P had to repay the money if the volume commitments were not met.

♦ In *Commissioner v. Indianapolis Power & Light Co.,* 493 U.S. 203 (1990), the Supreme Court ruled that utility customers' security deposits were not income because there was an obligation to repay the money when the services ended. In *Automobile Club of Michigan v. Commissioner*, 353 U.S. 180 (1957), pre-paid membership dues were income when received because a pro rata application of the dues to each month would not bear any relation to the services the club had to perform, and the taxpayer was entitled to keep the dues even if no services were requested.

♦ Here, the cash advance had to be repaid if volume requirements were not met. Therefore, this case is more like *Indianapolis Power* than *Automobile Club*. The fact that the amount of the repayment might be less than the total advance does not change the analysis or the outcome.

Comment. The decision in *Westpac* was based on tax accounting principles. The fact that generally accepted accounting principles require the cash to be reported as income when the volume requirements are met was immaterial. This decision clarifies the requirements for taxable income. A taxpayer must realize an increase in wealth and have complete control of the cash. An increase in wealth does not exist as long as there is an obligation to return the cash based on future performance or nonperformance.

---

6. **Reserves.** Many taxpayers, faced with the refusal of courts to permit deferment of unearned income, have attempted to offset the immediate inclusion of prepaid income by immediately deducting the costs which would be incurred in the future in earning that income. The accounting technique to accomplish this result is the use of "reserves" for estimated future expenses. However, these reserves have been held to be nondeductible.

7. **Deduction Items.**

   a. **The accrual concept.** An expense's deductibility occurs when all the events have occurred which establish an unconditional duty to pay and when the amount owing is reasonably ascertainable. [Treas. Reg. 1.461-1(a)(2)] The Tax Reform Act of 1984 added I.R.C. section 461(h). This section requires that economic performance occur before a liability can be accrued. Economic performance includes the rendering of services, providing property, or payment. [I.R.C. §461(h)(2)] If a taxpayer is disputing a claim that he owes payment, he cannot accrue the item as a deduction since he does not recognize an unconditional obligation. However, if the taxpayer does finally make payment even under protest, section 461 allows its deductibility as an expense.

   b. **The deferral concept.** An expense, though paid, is not deductible under the accrual method if it is attributable to the earnings of a later accounting period. This in effect applies the capitalization concept to noncapitalizable expenditures.

I. CORPORATE TRANSACTIONS—INCORPORATION

1. **Introduction.** The formation of a corporation and the transfer to it of property in return for stock or securities is ordinarily not a transaction in which gain or loss is recognized. I.R.C. section 351 provides that no gain or loss shall be recognized if property is transferred to a corporation solely in exchange for its stock or securities, and if immediately after the exchange the transferor or transferors control the corporation. The policy is that formation of a corporation is not an appropriate time to collect a tax on the appreciation of assets which are being transferred to the corporation to be employed in

the new business. On the other hand, the taxpayer may wish to avoid the effect of section 351 where the assets being transferred have depreciated in value and would generate a loss if the transaction were held to constitute a taxable "sale."

2. **Qualifying Under Section 351.**

   a. **Control.** In order to qualify for nonrecognition of gain under section 351, the transferors of property to the corporation must, as a group, have control of the corporation "immediately after the transfer." This means that they must own at least 80% of the voting stock and 80% of each other class of stock. [I.R.C. §§351(a), 368(c)]

   b. **"Property."** Eligible property for a section 351 exchange includes cash, accounts receivable (including those with a "zero" basis), and intangible assets, but does not include services. However, if services are contributed with property, the contributor will be included fully for the 80% control requirement *supra,* but will recognize ordinary income for the amount of services contributed for stock or securities.

3. **Problems in the Incorporation of an Existing Business.** The transfer of an existing business often creates special section 351 problems.

   a. **Accounts receivable and bad debt reserves.** When an accrual taxpayer transfers accounts receivable with a bad debt reserve, there is no tax to the transferor if the value of the stock and securities received is not in excess of the net amount of the accounts receivable. [Nash v. United States, 398 U.S. 1 (1970)] Where the value is in excess of the net receivables, the transferor must recognize the difference as ordinary income.

   b. **Accounts payable.** Accounts receivable transferred by a cash basis taxpayer have a zero basis in the hands of the transferor (and thus in the hands of the corporation). The corporation thus reports income as it collects the receivables. Accounts payable would, on the other hand, be treated as deductible by the corporation.

   c. **Inventory.** Similarly, the transfer of inventory items from a cash basis taxpayer (where the expenses associated with inventory would have been deducted) to a corporation results in a zero basis in the hands of the corporation. Sale of these items then generates ordinary income.

   d. **Depreciable property.**

      1) **I.R.C. section 1239.** Taxpayers with assets having a low basis but high value may wish to get a stepped-up basis in the assets in the hands of the corporation (to get high depreciation). The trade-off

between taking a capital gain on the transfer and the higher depreciation in the corporation is normally a profitable one only where the life of the asset is short. Section 1239, which is applicable to sales between a corporation and an 80% shareholder (counting the shares the shareholder controls), meets this problem by treating the gain on sale as ordinary income rather than capital gain.

2) **Recapture of depreciation and investment credit.** I.R.C. sections 1245(b)(3) and 1250(d)(3) provide that there is no recapture of depreciation in section 351 transactions except to the extent that there is gain recognized by section 351. Also, under the regulations there is no recapture of the investment credit (if the tests of the regulations are met).

4. **Examples of Section 351 Transactions:**

a. X and Y form a corporation (A). X transfers $100,000 cash and Y transfers land worth $100,000 to A. Both receive 100 shares of stock. Y's basis in the land is $30,000. Y's gain is not recognized. A has a $30,000 basis in the land. X's basis in the stock is $100,000.

b. If X gave a promise to render future services rather than cash, X would have ordinary income of $100,000. Y would have to recognize $70,000 gain on the land. A's basis in the land would be $100,000. The basis of both X and Y in their stock would be $100,000.

c. If X gives cash and Y land, and Y receives stock plus a promissory note for $40,000 due in three years, then the note is "boot" (and probably not a "security"). Y would recognize gain up to the amount of the boot ($40,000). A's basis would be $70,000 (Y's old basis, plus gain recognized). Y's basis for his stock would be $30,000 (basis for land, minus boot, plus gain recognized). Y's basis for the note would be $40,000.

d. In the previous paragraph, if the promissory note had been for 10 years, then probably it would be a security. Y would not recognize any gain and A's basis would be only $30,000. Y would allocate his $30,000 basis over the stock and the security (based on their proportional fair market values).

J. CORPORATE TRANSACTIONS—REORGANIZATIONS

I.R.C. section 61(a)(3) provides that the term "gross income" includes "gains derived from dealings in property." I.R.C. section 165(a) provides that losses, with certain limitations, may be taken as deductions. To be taxable as gain, or deductible as a loss, a "realizable event" must occur with respect to the taxpayer's property. Unrealized appreciation or depreciation in the value of property does not constitute a taxable transaction. When there is a realizable event, then the amount of gain or loss is determined under I.R.C. section 1001, which provides that the taxpayer's gain or loss is the difference between the "amount realized" for the property and its adjusted basis. I.R.C. section 1002 provides that this "realized" gain or loss must be recognized, unless otherwise provided by the Code. One group of these situations occurs in I.R.C. sections 354 through 368 (the corporate reorganization provisions). The underlying assumption of these provisions is that the new company is substantially a continuation of the old enterprise. This continuation is the reason why gain or loss, although realized, is not recognized.

IV. PERSONAL DEDUCTIONS, EXEMPTIONS, AND CREDITS

A. INTRODUCTION

A number of items are deductible even though they have no relationship to a business or investment. These include interest, state and local taxes (except sales taxes), medical expenses, charitable contributions, and casualty losses.

B. THE STANDARD DEDUCTION

Some deductions, such as those for business expenses, are allowed in reducing *gross* income to adjusted gross income. Other deductions, such as interest, taxes, contributions, and medical expenses, are allowed to reduce *adjusted* gross income to taxable income. Taxpayers may elect to take a standard deduction in lieu of this latter group of deductions. This option is advantageous to the wage earner who does not own a mortgaged home or make extensive contributions. For 2009, the standard deduction is $11,400 on a joint return and $5,700 for unmarried individuals. These amounts are increased in future years to reflect increases in the Consumer Price Index. The standard deduction is increased in each instance if the taxpayer is at least 65 years of age or blind.

C. CASUALTY LOSSES

1. **Introduction.** I.R.C. section 165(c)(3) allows deductions for personal losses arising from "fire, storm, shipwreck, or other casualty or from theft."

2. **What Is a Casualty?**

   a. **Suddenness.** A "casualty" has been defined as "an accident, a mishap, some sudden invasion by a hostile agency. It excludes the progressive deterioration of property through a steadily operating cause." [Fay v. Helvering, 120 F.2d 253 (2d Cir. 1941)]

   b. **Termite damage.** Rev. Rul. 63-232 states that termite damage to non-business property is not deductible as a casualty loss under I.R.C. section 165(c)(3).

3. **Limitations Resulting from Recent Legislation.** Currently, casualty and theft losses are deductible only to the extent that the total casualty losses for the year exceed 10% of adjusted gross income. Each casualty loss must (as under prior law) be reduced by $100. Also, no loss will be allowed if taxpayers do not file timely insurance claims on losses covered by insurance.

4. **The Meaning of "Other Casualty"--**

Dyer v. Commissioner, 20 T.C.M. 705 (1961).

Facts. Dyer (P) owned two matched vases having a combined value of $250, each of which was worth $100. One of the vases was broken when P's Siamese cat knocked it over while having a neurotic fit. P's insurance refused to pay for the vase, and P claimed a $100 casualty loss for its breakage. The Commissioner (D) argued that a loss caused by a cat does not qualify under section 165(c)(3) as a casualty loss. P paid a deficiency and brought suit for a refund.

Issue. Does a property loss caused by a sudden illness of a pet qualify as an "other casualty" under section 165?

Held. No.

♦ The rule of ejusdem generis applies here. Losses caused by fire, storm, shipwreck, or other like-kind occurrences qualify for casualty losses. None of the like occurred in this case.

---

5. **Temporary Casualty--**

Chamales v. Commissioner, T.C. Memo 2000-33.

Facts. The Chamales (Ps) contracted to buy a home next door to the home owned by O.J. Simpson in Brentwood, California, shortly before the murders of Nicole Brown Simpson and Ronald Goldman. Unprecedented attention by the media and celebrity hounds continued for months. On their 1994 income tax return, Ps characterized these events as a casualty which permanently devalued their property and took a section 165(c)(3), I.R.C., casualty loss deduction of $751,427. The Commissioner (D) disallowed the deduction and imposed an I.R.C. section 6662(a) accuracy-related penalty on account of negligence.

Issues.

(i) Are Ps entitled to a casualty loss deduction for fluctuation in the market value of their property?

(ii) Are Ps liable for the section 6662(a) accuracy-related penalty on account of negligence?

Held. (i) No. (ii) No.

- The homicides were not the sudden, unexpected, and unusual event that will qualify as a casualty within the meaning of section 165(c)(3). That section defines a casualty loss as a loss of property "not connected with a trade or business or a transaction entered into for profit, if such losses arise from fire, storm, shipwreck, or other casualty, or from theft." The loss is not limited to those caused by forces of nature. Section 165 regulations provide a loss must be both "evidenced by closed and completed transactions" and "fixed by identifiable events."

- It cannot be concluded that the claimed devaluation of Ps' property was the direct and proximate result of the type of casualty contemplated by section 165(c)(3). The murders were a sudden and unexpected exertion of force, but this force was not exerted upon Ps' property. The influx of the media was not on Ps' property. Ps' claim is based on months or years of ongoing public attention. Thus, the source of Ps' difficulties is more like a steadily operating cause than a casualty. Press and media attention continuing for months is not like a fire, storm, or shipwreck and is not properly classified as an "other casualty."

- We have traditionally held that only physical damage to, or permanent abandonment of, property is deductible under section 165. Ps have not established physical damage, and while they mentioned minor physical damage in an attachment to their tax return, they offered no substantiation for such losses.

- Further, Ps' circumstances do not reflect permanent devaluation or buyer resistance. Media attention has lessened following the murders. Brentwood residents are investing substantial sums in remodeling their homes. Ps' situation reflects a temporary fluctuation in value. A deduction based on market devaluation is contrary to existing law.

- Section 6662(a) and (b)(1) imposes an accuracy-related penalty of 20% of any underpayment that is attributable to negligence or disregard of rules or regulations. Negligence is defined in section 6662(c) as "any failure to make a reasonable attempt to comply with the provisions of this title"; case law defines it as "a lack of due care or the failure to do what a reasonable and ordinarily prudent person would do under the circumstances."

- However, the exception provided in section 6664(c)(1), "[n]o penalty shall be imposed under this part with respect to any portion of an underpayment if it is shown that there was a reasonable cause for such portion and that the taxpayer acted in good faith with respect to such portion," applies here.

- Here, Ps relied on advice of an expert tax preparer, which is a factor to be considered. In order for this factor to be given dispositive weight, the taxpayer claiming reliance on a professional such as an accountant must show, at minimum, that (i) the accountant was supplied with correct information and (ii) the incorrect return was a result of the accountant's error.

♦ Ps have sustained their burden of proof. Ps sought advice from a realtor and an accountant, who then discussed the matter with two additional brokers. Both Ps supplied the accountant with factual data related to the nature of the loss, and they made full disclosure rather than obscure the reasons for their deduction. There was no unreasonableness or imprudence on Ps' part that would support the imposition of the section 6662(a) accuracy-related penalty.

---

6. **Ordinary Versus Gross Negligence--**

Blackman v. Commissioner, 88 T.C. 677 (1987).

Facts. Blackman (P) was transferred by his employer from Maryland to South Carolina. His wife was dissatisfied with the move and returned with the children to their home in Maryland. When P returned to Maryland to work things out with his wife, he found she was living with another man. After a couple of altercations with his wife, P gathered some of his wife's clothes and set them on fire on the stove. P claims that he then took pots of water and completely doused the fire and departed the house. The house then burned to the ground. Firemen found clothes still lying on the stove. P was charged with arson and malicious mischief. P was ordered to serve 24 months' probation on an arson charge. P's insurance company refused to honor his insurance claim due to the cause of the fire. P claimed a casualty loss of $97,853 on his federal income tax return for his loss attributable to the destruction of his residence and its contents. The Commissioner (D) disallowed the deduction.

Issue. Is P allowed a casualty deduction for the fire that he started?

Held. No.

♦ It is well established that negligence is not a bar to the allowance of the casualty deduction. However, gross negligence will bar a deduction. Once a person starts a fire, he has an obligation to make extraordinary efforts to see that such fire is completely extinguished. P was guilty of gross negligence.

♦ P's actions violated Maryland's laws regarding arson and burning, and domestic violence. To allow P a deduction for his loss would frustrate public policy.

D. MEDICAL EXPENSES

1. **Introduction.** I.R.C. section 213 provides a limited deduction for amounts paid "for the diagnosis, cure, mitigation, treatment, or prevention of disease,

or for the purpose of affecting any structure or function of the body." In addition, the expense must be incurred for the care of the taxpayer, his or her spouse, or a dependent.

2. **Limitation.** Medical expenses, including amounts of drugs and insurance premiums, are deductible to the extent that they exceed 7.5% of adjusted gross income. [I.R.C. §213(a)(1)]

3. **Capital Expenditures.** If a capital improvement is prescribed by a physician, the taxpayer may deduct the excess of the cost of the item reduced by the amount the improvement increases the value of the taxpayer's property. Rev. Rul. 59-411 cites an installed elevator as an example.

4. **Drugs.**

   a. **In general.** Starting in 1984, the deduction for medicine or drugs is limited to prescription drugs or insulin. Previously, any kind of medicine could have been deducted.

   b. **Limitation.** Also beginning in 1984, the expenses for drugs no longer are reduced by 1% of adjusted gross income. Drug costs are simply added to all other medical expenses and medical insurance premiums. The entire figure is deductible only to the extent it exceeds 7.5% of adjusted gross income.

5. **Doctor Recommendation--**

Taylor v. Commissioner, 54 T.C.M. 129 (1987).

Facts. Due to a severe allergy, Taylor's (P's) doctor instructed him not to mow his lawn. P paid $178 to have his lawn mowed in 1982 and deducted the cost as a medical expense deduction. The Commission (D) disallowed the deduction.

Issue. Can P deduct amounts paid to someone else for mowing his lawn since the doctor instructed P not to do so?

Held. No. Judgment for D.

♦ Under I.R.C. section 262, deductions for personal, living, or family expenses are not allowed. However, section 213 authorizes a deduction for medical care expenses that are not compensated for by insurance.

♦ P bears the burden of proving that the expense of the lawn care is a medical expense, but he has cited no authority to support his position. Also, he has not shown why other family members could not mow his lawn.

♦ Doctor-recommended activities have been held not to constitute deductible medical expenses when they do not fall within the parameters of "medical care," and P has not met his burden of proof.

---

6. **Depreciation--**

Henderson v. Commissioner, T.C. Memo 2000-321.

Facts. The Hendersons (Ps) purchased a van in 1991 solely to transport their son, Bradley, who suffers from spina bifida and is confined to a wheelchair. In 1992, a doctor told Ps that it was necessary to purchase a wheelchair lift due to Bradley's worsening condition. Ps modified their van at the cost of $4,406. During 1994 and 1995, Ps used the van to transport Bradley to doctors and hospitals, to school, and whenever he accompanied them on trips. By 1994, Bradley was in a full body shell and Ps could not find anyone willing to take care of him. Ps were advised by their CPA to deduct the cost of the van and conversion at $5,500 per year for the 1991 through 1995 tax years. After an audit of Ps' 1994 and 1995 returns, the depreciation deduction for both years was denied. Ps appeal.

Issue. Is depreciation deductible as a medical expense under section 213?

Held. No.

♦ Section 213 provides: "There shall be allowed as a deduction the expenses paid during the taxable year . . . for medical care of the taxpayer, his spouse, or a dependent . . . to the extent that such expenses exceed 7.5% of adjusted gross income."

♦ We have previously addressed this issue and held that depreciation is not an "expense paid" within the meaning of the statute.

---

7. **Expenses Not Solely Related to Medical Care--**

Ochs v. Commissioner, 195 F.2d 692 (2d Cir. 1952).

Facts. Ochs's (P's) wife underwent a thyroidectomy which left her unable to speak above a whisper. Efforts to speak were painful and left her in a highly nervous state. Knowing that she suffered from cancer of the throat, and upon the advice of a physician, P and his wife decided to place their two children in boarding school so that she could have a smoother recovery. P deducted the $1,456 paid to put the children in day school and boarding school as a medical expense. The Commissioner (D) and the Tax Court disallowed the deduction as not being a medical expense under I.R.C. section 213. P appeals.

Issue. Is a taxpayer entitled to deduct boarding school costs incurred to aid in a parent's recovery from an operation?

Held. No. Judgment affirmed.

♦   Boarding school costs are nondeductible family expenses rather than medical expenses. Certain expenses made to benefit a certain family member often benefit other family members as well. In this case, the expenses were made necessary by the loss of the wife's services, and the only reason that P advances in arguing that they should be deductible is that his wife also received a benefit. To allow this would transform nondeductible family expenses into medical expenses.

Dissent. This expense fell within the category of "mitigation, treatment or prevention of disease" and it was for the "purpose of affecting a structure or function of the body." Had P sent his wife to a sanitarium rather than sending his children to boarding school, there is little doubt that such expense would be deductible as a medical cost.

---

8. **Living Expenses.**

     a.   **Introduction.** An expenditure must have a proximate relationship to medical care to be deductible. Food and lodging expenses are not deductible since they would be incurred whether or not the taxpayer is under medical care.

     b.   **Exception.** I.R.C. section 213(d)(2) provides that amounts paid for lodging (although not in a hospital) are considered amounts paid for medical care if care is provided by a doctor in a licensed hospital, and there is no significant element of personal pleasure, recreation, or vacation in the travel. The deductible amount cannot exceed $50 per individual per night and payments cannot be extravagant under the circumstances.

E.   CHARITABLE CONTRIBUTIONS

1.   **Introduction.** I.R.C. section 170(c) allows a taxpayer to deduct contributions made to any entity organized and operated predominantly for charitable, religious, scientific, literary, or educational purposes. This deduction

is limited to 50% of the individual taxpayer's adjusted gross income or 10% of a corporate taxpayer's taxable income. However, the excess may be carried over to successive tax years.

2. Gifts with Private Objectives or Benefits--

Ottawa Silica Co. v. United States, 699 F.2d 1124 (Fed. Cir. 1983).

Facts. Ottawa Silica Co. (P) was in the business of mining, processing, and marketing silica. It owned about 2,300 acres of land near Oceanside, California. Only 481 acres of this land had silica reserves. As years passed, it became apparent that the remaining land would be valuable for future residential or commercial development. In 1968, a school district approached officials of P asking for a donation of 50 acres of its land to build a high school. The site was contributed, and P claimed a charitable contribution of $415,000. The government (D) argued that the contribution should not be allowed since P obtained a substantial benefit in return for the donation of land. The Court of Claims held for D. P appeals.

Issue. If a donor receives a benefit which is more than incidental to the transfer of the property, can it deduct the transaction as a charitable contribution?

Held. No. Judgment affirmed.

♦   Cases indicate that a "substantial benefit" received in return for a contribution constitutes a quid pro quo, or in other words, a benefit greater than that which would inure to the general public from a transfer for charitable purposes. In this case, P received a required access road which connected a future development on its land to Mission Boulevard. Without such an access road (whose future appeared doubtful until the high school was approved), development of a subdivision on P's land would not be viable. This was a substantial benefit and not incidental to the transaction.

Comments.

♦   In *Singer Co. v. United States,* 449 F.2d 413 (Ct. Cl. 1972), a donation of Singer sewing machines to schools was not given charitable contribution treatment since a prime motivating factor in the donation was to encourage the students to use and purchase the sewing machines in the future.

♦   If a contribution is made for some future economic benefit rather than from "detached and disinterested generosity," it is not deductible. The courts are increasingly using the *Duberstein* "disinterested generosity" test to determine if a taxpayer expects to receive something in return for his contribution. However, in *Estate of Wardwell v. United States,* 301 F.2d 632 (8th Cir. 1962), an elderly person made a donation to a nursing home and shortly thereafter moved to the home and paid a lower rent due to his donor status. The court allowed the deduction since the donor's gift gave him no enforceable property right.

♦   In *Hernandez v. Commissioner*, 490 U.S. 680 (1989), the Supreme Court disallowed a deduction for amounts paid by members of the Church of Scientology for individual training courses. Since the payments were required of members attending the sessions, the members received an identifiable benefit from attending the sessions.

---

3.   **Qualification of Donees.**

   a.   **Introduction.** In order to qualify for a deduction, the taxpayer's contribution must be to a recognized charity. I.R.C. section 170(c) states that a contribution must be to a governmental or other entity organized and operated predominantly for charitable, religious, scientific, literary, or educational purposes. Charitable organizations are required to seek an eligibility determination from the IRS. This normally assures deductible status to the taxpayer's contribution.

   b.   **The public interest standard--**

Bob Jones University v. United States, 461 U.S. 574 (1983).

Facts. Bob Jones University (P) is a nonprofit institution with an enrollment of about 5,000 students from kindergarten through graduate school. The school claims to be "giving special emphasis to the Christian religion and the ethics revealed in the Holy Scriptures." Based on religious beliefs, P denies enrollment to unmarried blacks and blacks married interracially. Until 1970, the IRS (D) granted tax-exempt status to P, but later changed their policy and notified P that D would challenge the tax-exempt status of private schools practicing racial discrimination. This appeal results from a tax assessment for the years 1971 through 1975. The court of appeals upheld D's denial of tax exemption and P appeals.

Issue. Is an educational institution which practices racial discrimination tax-exempt for federal income tax purposes?

Held. No. Judgment affirmed.

♦   When an exemption or deduction is granted, all other taxpayers are affected and become indirect "donors." To warrant exemption under I.R.C. section 501(c)(3), an institution must serve and be in harmony with the public interest.

♦   There is no doubt that racial discrimination in education violates deeply and widely held views of elementary justice and is contrary to public policy.

♦ The IRS has the responsibility, in the first instance, to determine whether an entity is "charitable." This in turn may necessitate a determination of whether given activities so violate public policy as to jeopardize tax-exempt status.

♦ Legislative acquiescence and refusal to adopt numerous bills meant to overturn the IRS's interpretation of section 501(c)(3) illustrate congressional approval of a public interest standard.

♦ Denial of tax benefits does not amount to violation of a private religious school's right to observe its religious tenets.

Concurrence (Powell, J.). The critical question here is not whether an organization confers a public benefit. Such a policy, encouraging only governmentally approved policies, discourages diverse and conflicting activities and viewpoints.

Dissent (Rehnquist, J.). Congress's failure to act on this question does not empower the IRS to act for it. Organizations which provide a public benefit were intended to be given tax-exempt status under I.R.C. section 501(c)(3). However, this does not warrant a burden that the organization must show that its activity must serve and be in harmony with the public interest.

---

4. **Donated Services and Free Use of Property.** The value of personal services donated to a charity is not deductible. [Treas. Reg. 1-170-2(a)(2)] Also, if a taxpayer allows a charity to use his property rent-free, he may not deduct the value of the forgone rent as a charitable deduction. However, a taxpayer's out-of-pocket expenses in aiding a charity are deductible.

5. **Contributions of Appreciated Property.**

   a. **Prior law.** Before the Tax Reform Act of 1969, a taxpayer could deduct the fair market value of property donated to charity. This gave the taxpayer the advantage of deducting the full value of the property without having to recognize a gain for the appreciation.

   b. **Present law.** The taxpayer may still deduct the fair market value of donated property if that property would, if sold, produce long-term capital gain. This deduction is limited to 30% of the donor's adjusted gross income. Gifts of property in excess of $5,000 (except publicly traded stock) must be substantiated and an appraisal attached to the tax return.

      1) **Non-long-term capital gain property.** The taxpayer who donates short-term capital gain or ordinary income property may only claim a charitable deduction not to exceed *his basis* in the property. This deduction is reduced further by any depreciation that would have been recaptured had the property been sold.

6. **Bargain Sales.** When a taxpayer sells property to a charitable organization for a price below its fair market value, the difference is deductible as a charitable contribution.

7. **Contribution for Consideration.** In Rev. Rul. 86-63, 1986-1 C.B. 88, the IRS ruled that contributions to university athletic programs that entitle the donor to purchase tickets are deductible only to the extent that the contribution exceeds the value of the benefit. The 1988 tax act adopted I.R.C. section 170(m). This section allows a deduction of 80% of any amount paid to a university athletic program if the deduction would be deductible but for the fact that the taxpayer receives the right to purchase tickets for seating at an athletic event.

F. INTEREST

1. **Introduction.** I.R.C. section 163 allows the taxpayer to deduct certain interest payments. Prior to the Tax Reform Act of 1986, all interest, both personal and business, was deductible. However, beginning in 1987, the only personal interest that is deductible is home mortgage interest. Other personal interest was phased out over a five-year period.

   a. **What is interest?** Payments for the use of money qualify as interest. These could be thought of as rental payments for the use of money. However, service charges for the lender's services are not deductible as interest.

      1) **Points.** Some lenders charge an additional "loan processing fee" (points) when loaning money. These charges are considered payments for the use of money and are deductible as interest.

   b. **Limitations.** Interest incurred in a trade or business will be fully deductible. Interest incurred in acquiring investments will be deductible only to the extent of net investment income. Home mortgage interest will be deductible on a first and second residence. Qualified residence interest can fall within two categories. First, there is acquisition indebtedness for the purchase or improvement on a personal residence. This amount of debt is limited to $1 million. Second, there is home equity debt which is any debt secured by a residence with a limit of $100,000, but not in excess of the fair market value of the residence.

   c. **Comment.** Taxpayers can obtain second mortgages (subject to the limitations) and pay off nondeductible personal loans. In addition, the second mortgage loan proceeds can be used to purchase other personal items.

   d. **Tax-exempt interest.** Interest on debt used to purchase tax-exempt state or municipal bonds is not deductible. [I.R.C. §265(2)] However, to disallow this deduction, some purposeful connection must exist between the funds borrowed and the investment. [Wisconsin Cheeseman v. United States, 338 F.2d 420 (7th Cir. 1968)]

    e.   **Tracing.** Treasury Regulation section 1.163-8T provides rules for tracing interest to determine to which category of interest it belongs.

G. TAXES

I.R.C. section 164 allows every taxpayer to deduct various kinds of state and local taxes, including income taxes, real and personal property taxes, and gasoline taxes. Also, a taxpayer may deduct certain taxes paid in connection with his business or investment, which would otherwise not be deductible. These include excise taxes and Social Security taxes paid on employees. However, certain types are never deductible. These include federal income taxes, federal estate and gift taxes, and state inheritance taxes.

H. PERSONAL AND DEPENDENCY EXEMPTIONS

1.   **Personal Exemptions.** In 2008, individual taxpayers were allowed a personal exemption of $3,500. However, individuals claimed as dependents by another taxpayer were not entitled to the exemption.

2.   **Dependency Exemptions.** An exemption may be claimed by the taxpayer for each qualifying dependent. To qualify, five tests must be met:

    a.   **Gross income test.** The dependent's gross income must be less than $3,500 unless he is under 19 or a student. [I.R.C. §151(e)]

    b.   **Support test.** The taxpayer must supply over one-half of the dependent's support. [I.R.C. §152(a)]

    c.   **Relationship test.** The dependent must either be a close relative of the taxpayer or have his principal place of residence with the taxpayer. [I.R.C. §152(a)]

    d.   **Citizenship or residence.** The dependent must have been a citizen or resident of the United States, a resident of Canada or Mexico, or an alien adopted by, and living the entire year with, a United States citizen in a foreign country.

    e.   **Married dependent.** The dependent cannot have filed a joint return. However, if neither the dependent nor his spouse is required to file, but file a joint return anyway to get a refund or tax withheld from wages, the dependent can be claimed.

3. **Divorce and Dependency Exemptions.** If a couple divorces and they have children, I.R.C. section 152(e)(1) provides that the parent having custody of the child for the majority of the year gets the dependency exemption. However, the parties can agree in writing to give the exemption to the parent with custody for less than half the year if that parent pays at least $600 in child support during the year. Such agreements are modifiable under certain circumstances.

   a. **Application to parents who never married--**

King v. Commissioner, 121 T.C. 12 (2003).

Facts. Mrs. King (P) and Mr. Lopez are the biological parents of Monique, born in 1986. Lopez and P were never married. Monique lived with her mother, who completed and signed form 8332, granting the dependency exemption to Lopez for 1987 and all future years. Lopez claimed the exemption for those years. Beginning in 1993, P and her husband also claimed Monique as a dependent. In 2002, the Commissioner (D) disallowed the exemptions for both taxpayers for 1998 and 1999 to protect the government from being whipsawed. P and Lopez lived apart for all of 1998 and 1999, and the child lived with P at all times during the two years. P and her husband filed a petition with the Tax Court for relief, as did Lopez and his wife. The Tax Court consolidated the two cases.

Issue. Is P entitled to the dependency exemption deduction for Monique?

Held. No. Lopez and his wife are entitled to the exemption.

♦ A child of a taxpayer is generally a dependent of the taxpayer only if the taxpayer provides over half of the child's support during the taxable year. The parent having custody for a greater portion of the calendar year is considered as providing over half of the child's support for that year and is entitled to the dependency exemption. However, if the custodial parent signs a valid written declaration that she will not claim the child as a dependent for a taxable year, and the noncustodial parent attaches the written declaration to his tax return for the taxable year, the noncustodial parent gains entitlement to the deduction. The declaration may apply to one year, a set number of years, or all future years.

♦ P and D argued that the special support test of section 152(e)(1) applied only to taxpayers who had been previously married and that P should be allowed the exemption since she had provided over 50% of Monique's support. The Tax Court disagreed. It said that the statute's plain language meant that it applied to any parents who lived apart for the last six months of the tax year and who, together or individually, provided more than 50% of their child's support. Despite the specific language of section 152(e)(1), D argued that Congress intended the provision to apply only to parents who previously had been married to each other. The Tax Court also rejected this argument. It examined the legislative history and found nothing to indicate such intent. P validly released her claim to the exemption deductions for Monique for the years at issue.

I. CREDITS

1. **The Earned Income Tax Credit.** The Earned Income Tax Credit ("EITC") provides a refundable federal income tax credit for poor working individuals and families. Originally approved in 1975, when the EITC exceeds the amount of taxes owed, it results in a tax refund to those who claim and qualify for the credit. The EITC amount is determined by income and family size. To qualify for the credit in 2008, both the earned income and the adjusted gross income for 2008 had to have been less than $33,995 for a taxpayer with one qualifying child ($36,995 for married filing jointly), $38,646 for a taxpayer with more than one qualifying child ($41,646 for married filing jointly), and $12,880 for a taxpayer with no qualifying children. For 2008, some employees with at least one child living with them may be entitled to receive advance EITC payments in their paychecks. The employer receives advance payments and then pays part of the credit to the employee in advance throughout the year. The taxpayer claims the rest when filing the 2008 federal tax return. The EITC does not generally affect eligibility for Medicaid, Supplemental Security Income ("SSI"), food stamps, or low-income housing. [I.R.C. §32]

2. **Credit for Adoption Expenses.** A credit up to $11,650 is provided for adoption expenses for each child adopted. The credit is nonrefundable; *i.e.*, it reduces taxes to zero but not below. However, if a credit exceeds one's income tax liability, the excess credit can be carried forward for five years. In addition, the adoption credit can now reduce both your regular tax and your Alternative Minimum Tax. [I.R.C. §23]

3. **Child Tax Credit.** Certain taxpayers with dependent children are entitled to a tax credit on their federal income tax return. The credit is granted for each qualifying child. The credit is phased out (not permitted) for upper income taxpayers. The 2003 Tax Act increased the child tax credit from $600 to $1,000 for each qualifying child.

V. ALLOWANCES FOR MIXED BUSINESS AND PERSONAL OUTLAYS

A. INTRODUCTION

Congress allows the deduction of substantially all expenses incurred in the taxpayer's trade, business, or profit-seeking transactions. Unlike the cost of living, the cost of earning a living is deductible. Therefore, in determining whether a loss or an expense item is deductible, the item must first be characterized—either it was incurred in business or profit-seeking activity (deductible) or it is an item of personal expense (not deductible unless it comes under one of the specific statutory exceptions discussed *supra*).

1. Statutory Framework.

a. Ordinary and necessary expenses. Section 162(a) provides for the deduction of all ordinary and necessary expenses paid or incurred during the tax year in carrying on any trade or business. However, I.R.C. section 183 limits these deductions to activities engaged in for profit.

b. Production of income. Section 212 provides for the deduction of all ordinary and necessary expenses paid or incurred during the tax year for the collection or production of income or for the management, conservation, or maintenance of property held for the production of income, or in connection with the determination, collection, or refund of any tax. This section has been construed to include an individual's profit-seeking activities in real estate, investment in stocks and bonds, or in any other profit-seeking activities.

c. Deduction of losses. Section 165(a) provides for the deduction of losses not compensated for by insurance or otherwise. Sections 165(c)(1) and (2) apply to individuals and restrict deductions to losses incurred in a trade or business or in a transaction entered into for profit (such as from the sale of securities), except for casualty losses (discussed at IV.C., *supra*) over $100.

B. CONTROLLING THE ABUSE OF BUSINESS DEDUCTIONS

1. Hobby Losses.

a. Introduction. A taxpayer may deduct only the losses of a *profit-seeking* activity. An activity is presumed to be for profit-making purposes if, for at least two of the last five taxable years, the activity brought the taxpayer a net profit. Otherwise, the facts and circumstances are explored to ascertain the taxpayer's intent. If the losses were sustained in a nonprofit-seeking activity, the taxpayer may deduct interest, taxes, and other costs not to exceed the income produced from the investment.

b.   **Taxpayer profit motive--**

Nickerson v. Commissioner, 700 F.2d 402 (7th Cir. 1983).

Facts. Nickerson (P) grew up on his family's farm. After spending some years of his life in the advertising business, he and his wife began looking for alternative sources of income. They purchased 120 acres of farmland in Wisconsin. The farm was in a run-down condition and had little equipment that was not either in disrepair or obsolete. P leased the farm to a tenant-farmer for $20 per acre with the agreement that the tenant would cultivate an additional 10 acres of land with a profitable crop. P visited the farm most weekends during the growing season and twice a month during the rest of the year. Each trip required five hours of driving between his home in Chicago and the farm. P did not expect to earn a profit from the farm for about 10 years. P lost $8,668 in 1976 and $9,873 in 1977. He did not keep a formal set of books but kept a record of receipts and canceled checks. The Tax Court held that the facts did not support P's claim that his primary goal in operating the farm was to make a profit. P appeals.

Issue. Was the Tax Court's finding that P's motivation was other than to make a profit in operating the farm erroneous?

Held. Yes. Judgment reversed.

♦   Section 183 of the Code allows only ordinary and necessary business expenses when incurred for profit. To determine a profit motive, a court looks into the facts and circumstances of the activity. These include operating in a business-like manner, the expertise of the taxpayer in the business, the time and effort expended, and occasional profits earned by the activity.

♦   The Tax Court was incorrect in finding that P's primary goal in engaging in farming was not to make a profit. Although P and his wife did not expect to reap an immediate profit, they were motivated by the expectation that a later profit would accrue. Especially important here are the amount of time P devoted to working on the farm and the relationship which P had with the tenant-farmer, which tended to show a concrete plan to operate the farm.

Comment. Note that in this case the taxpayer was able to show a profit-seeking motive without passing the "two years out of five" presumption mentioned above.

---

2. Home Offices.

a. **Self-employed individuals.** Costs of a portion of a taxpayer's residence are deductible as a business expense if used exclusively for a principal place of business or dealing with patients, clients, or customers. [I.R.C. §280A(c)(1)]

b. **Employees.** Use of a residence as a business is deductible only if it is for the employer's convenience. This standard is very narrowly construed.

c. **Limitation.** The deductible portion is limited to the taxpayer's gross income reduced by nonbusiness allowed deductions such as real estate taxes and interest.

d. **Professional musician--**

Popov v. Commissioner, 246 F.3d 1190 (9th Cir. 2001).

Facts. Popov (P), a professional violinist, performed regularly with an orchestra and a symphony and, in 1993, contracted with 24 contractors to record music for the motion picture industry in 38 different locations. The recording sessions required that P read scores quickly because she did not get the sheet music until she arrived at the studio shortly before the actual recording began. P was not provided a place to practice by any of her employers. P used the living room of her one-bedroom apartment, which she shared with her husband and daughter, as a home office. The furniture in the room was only for P's music, her practice and recording equipment. The child was not permitted to play in the room and no one slept there. P practiced there four to five hours a day. On their 1993 return, P and her husband claimed the room as a home office and deducted 40% of their rent and 20% of their electricity costs. The Commissioner (D) disallowed the deductions, and Ps filed a petition for redetermination. The Tax Court disallowed the deduction; Ps appeal.

Issue. Is a professional musician entitled to deduct the expenses from the portion of her home used exclusively for musical practice?

Held. Yes. Judgment reversed.

♦ Section 280A(c)(1)(A) permits a deduction for a home office that is exclusively used as "the principal place of business for any trade or business of the taxpayer, but does not define "principal place of business."

♦ The Supreme Court addressed this issue most recently in *Commissioner v. Soliman*, 506 U.S. 168 (1993), in which the Court denied a home office deduction for an anesthesiologist who worked with patients 30 to 35 hours a week at three different hospitals, none of which provided him with an office. Soliman used a spare bedroom to contact patients and doctors, maintain records, prepare for treatment and read medical journals. The Court said that, although the use of a home office may be legitimate, it must be determined whether it is the taxpayer's principal place of business. No formula was offered for application in every case, but the Court emphasized "the relative importance of the activities performed at each business location and the time spent at each place."

♦ Regular daily practice is vital to P's professional career. Concert halls and studios are also important. In *Soliman*, the Court stated that, even though no one test is determinative, "the point where goods and services are delivered must be given great weight in determining the place where the most important functions are performed." We reject D's contention that P's performances in concert halls and studios are similar to Soliman's delivering anesthesia. Rendering music cannot be easily wrenched into a "delivery of services" characterization. Carried further, Ds would suggest that an attorney's primary place of business is the podium from which he delivers his oral argument, or that a professor's primary place of business is the classroom, rather than the office in which he prepares his lectures. Comparing the importance of the functions performed at various places provides no definitive answer in this case.

♦ Here, comparing the amount of time spent at home with the time spent at other places where business activities occur becomes very significant. Soliman spent much more time at the hospitals than in his home office. P spends more time practicing than performing or recording. This is the factor that allows the deduction; the office was exclusively used as her principal place of business.

♦ The Second Circuit agreed in *Drucker v. Commissioner*, 715 F.2d 67 (2d Cir. 1983), a case involving concert musicians employed by the Metropolitan Opera Association. No practice space was provided them and each musician used a part of his or her apartment to study music and to practice for approximately 30 hours a week. The Second Circuit reversed the Commissioner's and the Tax Court's denial of a home office deduction, rejecting the Tax Court's contention that practice was not a requirement or condition of employment. It found that home practice was the "focal point" of the appellant musicians' employment-related activities.

---

3. **Vacation Homes.**

   a. **General rule.** I.R.C. section 280A provides that the allowable deductions associated with a dwelling used as a personal residence are limited to those otherwise deductible. These would include interest and property taxes. Use as a personal residence is defined as personal use of the unit the greater of either 14 days or 10% of the days it is rented. To illustrate the allocation rules of I.R.C. section 280A, assume these facts for the following examples: The taxpayer rented a vacation home for 91 days and occupied it for personal use 32 days, for a total of 121 days used. Interest and taxes were $3,475 and maintenance costs were $2,693. Rental income is $2,700.

b. **Maintenance costs.** I.R.C. section 280A(c)(3) further allows deduction of maintenance expenses attributable to the rental of the unit. The amount deductible is the pro rata portion attributable to days rented vis-a-vis the total days the unit was used. In this example the deductible portion of the maintenance expense would be:

91 days rented/121 total days used X $2,693 = $2,020

c. **Limitation.** I.R.C. section 280A(c)(5) provides that the deduction allocable to the rental of the unit (including interest, taxes, and maintenance) cannot exceed the rental income from the unit. Interest and taxes are allocated according to the number of days rented divided by 365. In this example the interest ($2,854) and taxes ($621) of $3,475 allocable to the rental portion is:

91 days rented/365 X $3,475 = $868

d. **Example.** The above two calculations show the amount of deductible maintenance expense to be:

$2,700   gross income
- 868   allocable interest and taxes
$1,832   of $2,020 maintenance expense is deductible

4. **Income Unconnected to a Trade or Business.**

a. **Investment activities--**

Moller v. United States, 721 F.2d 810 (Fed. Cir. 1983).

Facts. Mr. and Mrs. Moller (P) had investment portfolios valued at over $13 million in 1976 and 1977. They managed their investments, spending approximately 40 to 42 hours a week tracking their stocks and bonds. Their investments focused on the long-term growth potential and the payment of interest and dividends. Most stocks sold were held more than three and one-half years. P claimed a deduction in 1976 and 1977 for an office in the home for both their office in their summer home and their office in their winter home. These offices were used exclusively for their investment activities. The IRS (D) disallowed P's office in the home deduction. P filed suit in the Claims Court. The Court held that P was an investor, not a trader, but was nevertheless engaged in the trade or business of making investments and was entitled to the deduction. D appeals.

Issue. Can an investor qualify for a trade or business office in the home deduction?

Held. No. An investor cannot take an office in the home deduction.

Comment. The court agreed that the Mollers actively engaged in managing their investments. However, since they were not in the market to make short-term gains from market fluctuations, they were not traders. Traders may be involved in a trade or business, while investors cannot.

---

b.   **Expenses incurred in participating in a game show--**

Whitten v. Commissioner, T.C. Memo. 1995-508.

Facts. In 1990, the taxpayer (P) passed a screening test in Chicago to be a contestant on the "Wheel of Fortune" television game show. In 1991, P flew his wife and three children to Los Angeles so that he could compete on Wheel of Fortune. P won three consecutive games and was awarded cash prizes in the amount of $14,850 and a 1991 Geo Tracker. On P's federal income tax return he reported his game show winnings as $19,830, the value of his winnings reduced by $1,820 for transportation, meals, and lodging incurred in order to participate as a contestant on the game show. The Commissioner (D) issued a deficiency notice determining that P failed to report $1,820 of his game show winnings. P claims that the expenses represent "gambling losses" that may be offset directly against P's "gambling winnings" from the program.

Issue. Are expenses incurred by the taxpayer to engage in the underlying wagering activity "gambling losses" that may offset "gambling winnings"?

Held. No.

♦   Gambling losses are amounts lost in a bet or wager. Congress did not intend for casual gamblers to be able to deduct miscellaneous expenses for meals, transportation, and lodging. These items should be treated as miscellaneous itemized deductions subject to the 2% floor or as nondeductible personal expenses.

---

5.   **Expenses and Losses Incurred in Business and Profit-Seeking Activities.** Section 262 states that "no deduction shall be allowed for personal, living, or family expenses." Since a person can make the same expenditure for both business and personal motives, the line between the two is sometimes hard to draw. A corporate taxpayer's expenses are presumed to have been incurred in connection with its trade or business, **unless** the outlay is

for the personal benefit of the shareholders. An individual taxpayer, however, must show that the *predominant purpose* of an expense was to fulfill business needs, not personal needs.

a.   **Personal versus business expense--**

Henderson v. Commissioner, 46 T.C.M. 566 (1983).

Facts. Henderson (P) was employed by the state of South Carolina as an assistant attorney general. As an employee, she was furnished with basic office furniture such as a desk, chair, telephone, law books, etc. During 1977, P purchased a framed print for $35, a plant for $35, and paid $180 rent for parking fees. The Commissioner (D) disallowed the losses as nondeductible personal expenses.

Issue. Are expenses incurred on office decorations and parking deductible?

Held. No. These expenses were personal in nature and only tangentially, if at all, aided her in her performance of her duties.

6.   **Automobiles and Computers.**

a.   **General rule.** The use of business automobiles and computers is covered by the "listed property" rules. The listed property rules provide that if such property is used 50% or less for business purposes, investment tax credits are not allowed and the taxpayer must use straight line depreciation methods. Moreover, if an employee purchases listed property such as a computer for home use, claiming that it was purchased for the convenience of the employer, he must exceed the 50% business use test or not get any deduction. [Rev. Rul. 86-129]

C.   TRAVEL AND ENTERTAINMENT EXPENSES

1.   **Introduction.** I.R.C. section 162 allows a travel expense deduction if incurred away from home in the pursuit of a trade or business. I.R.C. section 274(a) allows deduction of entertainment or recreation expenses only if directly related to the active conduct of business. Costs of socializing at nightclubs, casinos, and sporting events are deductible only if they immediately precede or follow a substantial and bona fide business discussion.

2.   **Conventions and Trips Paid for by Employer--**

Rudolph v. United States, 370 U.S. 269 (1962).

Facts. Rudolph (P) and his wife made a one-week trip to New York, which was paid for by P's employer. One morning was spent in a business meeting, with the remainder spent sightseeing by P. The Commissioner (D) claimed that the trip was a bonus to P and should have been included in his income. The district court and court of appeals agreed with D. P appeals.

Issue. Was the value of P's trip includable in gross income?

Held. Yes. Judgment affirmed.

- ◆ P claims that the trip is a "fringe benefit" not specifically excluded from section 61, but not intended to be within its reach. However, the trip is in the nature of a reward or bonus and should be included as gross income.

- ◆ The purpose of the trip was primarily personal in nature (*i.e.*, for P's enjoyment) rather than for business purposes.

Dissent (Douglas, Black, JJ.). P was expected to attend the convention which was geared to benefit the employer. Benefits which promote health, contentment, education, or goodwill are not "wages" to employees.

Comment. The costs of trips are not deductible unless they are made primarily for business, rather than personal purposes.

---

3. **Foreign Conventions.** The Tax Reform Act of 1976 added section 274(h), which restricts deductions for conventions held outside of the United States to two per year. The taxpayer must spend at least one-half of the days in business activities and attend at least two-thirds of the business activities of the convention. Subsistence expenses may not be deducted unless there are at least six hours of business activities scheduled; or, if there are at least three hours scheduled and the taxpayer attends at least two-thirds of those activities, half of the subsistence expenses may be deducted.

4. **Commuting Expenses.** Expenses incurred in traveling between the taxpayer's residence and his place of work are not deductible as business expenses.

5. **Living Away from Place of Business.** A taxpayer's travel expenses and expenses of living away from home are deductible if it is reasonable for the taxpayer to maintain a residence a distance from his trade or business. If a place of employment is in another city, it is reasonable to expect the taxpayer to change his residence to be near his new place of employment. Also, if a taxpayer, having a principal place of employment in one location, accepts work at another location which is not temporary but is of an indefinite or indeterminate period, his presence at the second location is not regarded

as "away from home." However, if a taxpayer accepts *temporary* work at a second location, this is regarded as being away from home. Hence, travel and living expenses incurred therein are deductible. See the cases discussed in E., *infra*.

6. **Meals.** The IRS allows deductions for meals purchased away from home if the taxpayer's travel involved a stop for sleep or rest. In *Barry v. Commissioner,* 435 F.2d 1290 (1st Cir. 1970), the taxpayer took long one-day trips and would stop by the side of the road for a nap during these trips. His claimed deduction for meals purchased during these trips was disallowed. The reason for the disallowance was that the taxpayer was not required to stop for rest as part of his employment. After 1993, only 50% of business meals and entertainment expenses are deductible beginning in 1987. In addition, in order to deduct the cost of a meal, the taxpayer must meet the general standards set forth for entertainment expenses: the taxpayer must be present and the meal must be related to the active conduct of a trade or business (or precede or follow a substantial and bona fide business discussion).

7. **Moving Expenses.** Section 217 allows employees or self-employed persons to deduct expenses for moving family and belongings to a new home. To qualify, the taxpayer's new job site must be over 35 miles farther from his old house than his old job site was. Also, he may not deduct over $1,500 for travel and temporary housing, nor over $3,000 for selling his old home and buying a new one. Since 1987, these expenses have been allowed only as itemized deductions from AGI (*i.e.*, "below the line" deductions).

8. **Business Entertainment.**

    a. **Entertainment facilities.** These are deductible if the taxpayer can show that the primary use of the facility was for ordinary and necessary business purposes, and the deduction is limited to this business use.

    b. **Recordkeeping.** Section 274(d) requires that the taxpayer keep adequate records and corroborative evidence supporting his entertainment expense claims. These are scrutinized carefully by the IRS and the courts. In *Levine v. Commissioner,* 51 T.C.M. 651 (1986), the taxpayer was denied a deduction for business entertainment for failing to substantiate any of the entertainment expenses. A similar conclusion was reached in *Carver v. Commissioner,* 50 T.C.M. 444 (1985), for failure to document business travel expenses.

    c. **Business lunches--**

Moss v. Commissioner, 758 F.2d 211 (7th Cir. 1985).

Facts. Moss (P) was a partner in a small trial firm. Each lawyer had a substantial caseload which required each of them to travel between the city and suburbs. Every weekday, the members met at the same restaurant near their office for lunch. At lunch, they would go over current cases and make assignments for the afternoon court call. P deducted his share of the cost of these lunches as a business expense. The Commissioner denied the deduction. P appeals.

Issue. Could P deduct the lunch meetings as an ordinary and necessary business expense?

Held. No. Judgment affirmed.

♦ Many expenses are simultaneously business and personal expenses. Lunch is a good example. Many people work and eat, thus producing income, but satisfying a personal need as well. However, for lunch to be deductible the expense must be different from or in excess of that which would have been made for the taxpayer's personal purposes. This most often occurs when the taxpayer takes someone out to lunch to get business or to persuade the person to join him in a business venture.

♦ The lunches here were different. While it may have been necessary to coordinate the firm's workload and that lunchtime was the optimum time to do this, it does not follow that this is a business expense. All the members had to eat somewhere. The restaurant was convenient, but none of the members claim a greater lunch expense than if they had each eaten alone and elsewhere. The meal itself was not a necessary part of achieving a business objective. Further, these meetings were only among lawyers participating in the firm. No new potential clients were brought to these meetings to secure new business. Consequently these lunches are a personal, not a business expense.

---

d.   Entertaining customers--

Danville Plywood Corp. v. United States, 899 F.2d 3 (1990).

Facts. Danville Plywood (P) manufactures custom plywood sold to wholesale distributors. On its 1980 and 1981 tax returns, P claimed $103,444.51 as a deduction for a weekend trip for 120 people to attend the Super Bowl in New Orleans. The people who went on the trip included employees and spouses, a shareholder's daughter, the president's children, the president's friends, P's customers, spouses and children of customers, and customers' customers. The weekend included accommodations, a dinner, an outing to the French Quarter, and the game. No official business meetings or discussions of any kind were scheduled. However, P had a display of its products in the hotel and instructed its employees to promote certain types of wood and survey the clients on their need for different types of products. Although no formal business meeting was held, P's employees met informally with customers during the weekend and circulated around the tables at dinner to speak with their guests. Upon audit, the Commissioner (D) disallowed the deductions related to the Super Bowl weekend. The Claims Court held for D. P appeals.

Issue. Do expenses incurred for a weekend trip to the Super Bowl qualify for a deduction as ordinary and necessary business expenses?

Held. No. Judgment affirmed.

♦ To be deductible, an entertainment expense must be an ordinary and necessary business expense under I.R.C. section 162 and be directly related to or associated with the trade or business under I.R.C. section 274. P failed to meet the first requirements of section 162, so further analysis of section 274 is not required. The costs associated with the children, the shareholder, and the employees' spouses were not deductible because these individuals did not perform a bona fide business purpose on the trip. The costs associated with the customers and their spouses were not deductible because the central focus of the trip was entertainment with an incidental amount of business discussions. Accordingly, the costs associated with P's employees were also not deductible because the trip was little more than a social excursion, with business playing a subsidiary role.

---

e. **Events for publicity--**

Churchill Downs, Inc. v. Commissioner, 307 F.3d 423 (6th Cir. 2002).

Facts. Churchill Downs, Inc. (P) owned several racetracks, and its biggest race was the Kentucky Derby. P held various dinners, parties, receptions, and galas for the press, VIPs, and others in connection with the Kentucky Derby and another race, the Breeders' Cup. The goal of these events was to maintain the image of P's businesses so they could compete for sports-event dollars. P deducted the entire cost of these social events as "ordinary and necessary" business expenses. The Commissioner (D) reduced P's deductions to 50% of the event costs under IRC section 274(n). P argued that since it was in the entertainment industry, "entertainment" was P's product and none of its entertainment costs should have been limited under section 274(n). The Tax Court found for D, and P appeals.

Issue. Are P's entertainment costs incurred to promote its entertainment business subject to the 50% entertainment limitation of section 274(n)?

Held. Yes. Judgment affirmed.

♦ The Court held that P's business was horse racing and the wagering thereon. While the events may have been necessary to publicize P's business, the events were not part of the product generated by P, and P did not make any money from hosting the events. P also failed to qualify for any exceptions under section 274 because its primary customers, the gaming public, were not allowed to attend the events.

D. CHILD CARE EXPENSES

1. Introduction--

Smith v. Commissioner, 40 B.T.A. 1038 (1939), *aff'd without opinion,* 113 F.2d 114 (2d Cir. 1940).

Facts. Smith (P) deducted the cost of paying a nursemaid to care for her children so she could work. She claimed that "but for" this expense, she would not be able to work. The Commissioner (D) disallowed the deduction.

Issue. Are child care costs deductible business expenses if, without incurring them, the taxpayer would be prevented from working?

Held. No. Judgment for D.

♦ These expenses fall under I.R.C. section 262 as a personal, living, or family expense. Their indirect connection with business pursuits does not cause them to become a business expense.

---

2. **Basic Statutory Law.** Deducting the cost of child care was traditionally not permitted as a business expense. However, Congress has provided a deduction for these costs (as a tax credit). A taxpayer can deduct from taxes owed up to 35% of the costs of caring for a dependent under age 15, plus household services, if the costs are incurred so that the taxpayer can be employed. The expense cannot exceed the earned income of the lower earning spouse (unless a student). The maximum credit is $3,000 for one child and $6,000 for two or more children. [*See* I.R.C. §21]

    a. **Formula applied.** The credit is reduced by one percentage point for each $2,000 (or fraction thereof) of income above $15,000. Thus, taxpayers with taxable income above $43,000 take a credit of 20% of eligible expenditures.

b. **Other limitations.** Expenses for out-of-home, noninstitutional care of a disabled spouse or dependent are made eligible for the credit, but expenditures at a child care center not in compliance with state or local regulations will not be eligible for the credit. Finally, amounts provided by an employer under a nondiscriminatory child care plan are not included in the employee's income.

E. COMMUTING EXPENSES

1. **Travel Expenses.** I.R.C. section 162(a)(2) allows the deduction of expenses for traveling, meals, and lodging while (i) "away from home," and (ii) in the "pursuit of a trade or business."

   a. **Pursuit of trade or business.** To be deductible, travel expenses must be primarily for business rather than personal reasons.

      1) **Business travel expense--**

Commissioner v. Flowers, 326 U.S. 465 (1946).

Facts. Flowers (P) was an attorney who lived in Jackson, Mississippi. His sole legal activity consisted of acting as general counsel for a railroad based in Mobile, Alabama, about 300 miles from Jackson. P made between 30 and 40 trips from his home to Mobile each year. P claimed a deduction for traveling expenses incurred on these trips in 1939 and 1940. The Commissioner (D) disallowed the deduction and the Tax Court affirmed his decision. The court of appeals reversed and D appeals.

Issue. Were P's traveling expenses required in carrying on his trade or business?

Held. No. Judgment reversed.

♦ The expenses were not incurred in the pursuit of the business of the taxpayer's employer. The expenses are nondeductible living costs which are unaltered by the distance which P lived from the post of many of his duties.

♦ Travel expenses are deductible only when the taxpayer's business forces him to travel and live away from home temporarily. Here P's frequent travel between Jackson and Mobile was not required by his employer but was occasioned by his personal preference to live away from his place of employment.

Dissent. The wording of the statute has been misconstrued, making understandable, ordinary English into highly technical tax jargon.

---

2) **Commuting expenses.** Costs of traveling between one's residence and place of work are not deductible. This is true even if the taxpayer commutes to and from a different place of business each day.

3) **Business travel expenses.** Unlike the costs of travel between a residence and business, the expense of traveling between places of business is deductible.

b. **Away from home.**

1) **Taxpayers with more than one home--**

Hantzis v. Commissioner, 638 F.2d 248 (1st Cir.), *cert. denied*, 452 U.S. 962 (1981).

Facts. Hantzis (P) was a law student who lived and attended school in Boston where her husband was a professor. After her second year of law school, she was unable to find a summer job as a clerk in Boston. She did find employment for 10 weeks in New York City. P's husband maintained their Boston residence while P lived in New York City during her summer job. P deducted the cost of her apartment, transportation, and meals in New York. The Commissioner (D) disallowed the deductions, but the Tax Court reversed. D appeals.

Issue. If a summer job requires maintenance of a second home, is this in pursuit of a trade or business?

Held. Only if the taxpayer has business reasons for maintaining both residences. Judgment reversed.

♦ The traveling expense deduction is not intended to exclude from taxation every expense incurred, in the course of business, for maintaining two homes. I.R.C. section 162(a)(2) requires that the two homes be maintained because of the exigencies of trade or business.

♦ The determining factor is the reason for maintenance of the two homes. If personal, then the deduction is denied. If the reason is business exigencies, then the deduction is allowed. Here P's trade or business did not require that she maintain a home in Boston as well as one in New York. Her visits to Boston during the summer were for personal reasons. P's choice to maintain two homes was a personal one, rather than one dictated by occupational necessity.

♦ The temporary employment doctrine does not apply here. Only if a taxpayer lives in one place and works in another where she has business ties to both will the deduction be allowed. P had no employment ties to Boston, only personal ones.

Concurrence. P was not required by her trade or business to maintain two homes. She had only personal, not business, ties to Boston.

Comment. A taxpayer with no permanent place of business will be allowed to treat his residence as his "home" for I.R.C. section 162 purposes. A transient worker (*i.e.*, one with no permanent business or residence) is not allowed a travel deduction.

----

2) **Temporary work assignments.** Rev. Rul. 83-82, 1983-2 C.B. 45, outlines the rules regarding away-from-home deductions. Generally, if a taxpayer is temporarily working away from his tax home for a year or less, it is presumed that such work is "away from home." If the work lasts between one and two years, the taxpayer must show that the work was temporary in nature. And, if the work lasts over two years, it is presumed to be indefinite and not a stay away from home.

F. CLOTHING EXPENSES

1. **General Rule.** The cost of clothing is a deductible business expense only if:

   a. The clothing is of a type specifically required as a condition of employment;

   b. The clothing is not adaptable to general usage as ordinary clothing; and

   c. The clothing is not generally used outside of employment by the taxpayer. [Donnelly v. Commissioner, 262 F.2d 411 (2d Cir. 1959)]

2. **Satisfying the Test--**

Pevsner v. Commissioner, 628 F.2d 467 (5th Cir. 1980).

Facts. Pevsner (P) was employed at an exclusive boutique whose only line of clothing was the expensive Yves St. Laurent (YSL) line. P was expected to wear YSL clothing at work and at fashion shows. In 1975, P purchased YSL clothing costing her $1,382 and expended another $240 in maintenance, both of which she claimed as a deduction. P argued that her simple and frugal lifestyle dictated that she not wear the YSL clothing away from her work, and in fact she only wore her YSL clothes at work. Stating that the apparel was not suitable to her private lifestyle, the Tax Court found for P. The Commissioner (D) appeals.

Issue. Are the YSL clothes worn by P deductible as an ordinary and necessary business expense?

Held. No. Judgment reversed.

♦ P did not wear the subject apparel outside of her employment. She was also specifically required as a condition of employment to wear the apparel at work. However, while the expensive clothing may not have been generally adaptable to P's lifestyle away from work, the test was not properly applied by the lower court. In determining general adaptability of work clothing, an objective (or generic) test should apply rather than a subjective view into each taxpayer's taste and lifestyle. This is an administrative necessity. YSL clothing is generally adaptable and is sold as ordinary clothing.

G. LEGAL EXPENSES

1. Divorce and Property Settlement--

United States v. Gilmore, 372 U.S. 39 (1963).

Facts. Gilmore (P) spent some $40,000 in defending against his wife's suit for divorce and alimony. P's overriding concerns in defeating the suit were in protecting his stock interests and automobile dealership from his wife's claims. P claimed a deduction for these expenses under section 212 as incurred for the "conservation . . . of property held for the production of income." The Commissioner (D) held the legal costs to be personal expenses. P filed a refund suit and the Court of Claims reversed D's ruling. D appeals.

Issue. Are legal expenses deductible if the litigant stands to lose income-producing assets if he loses the suit?

Held. No. Judgment reversed.

♦ The characterization of an expense as related to "business" or "personal" depends on whether the claim *arises in connection with* the taxpayer's profit-seeking activities. It does not depend on the *consequences* that might result to a taxpayer's income-producing property from a failure to defeat the claim.

♦ In this case the wife's claim stemmed entirely from the marital relationship, and not from income-producing activity.

Comment. Generally, a wife is allowed to deduct legal fees in collecting her alimony, since such income is treated on a par with the husband's profit-seeking activities. In a subsequent action, Gilmore was allowed to allocate his nondeductible legal expenses to the assets involved in the divorce suit, thereby increasing their basis.

---

2. **Expenses of Acquiring Property.** Normally, legal fees paid in connection with the acquisition of property are treated as capital items, not deductible expenses. For example, A buys property for $10,000. His neighbor claims that he owns 10 feet of the property; A then pays him $2,000 for a quitclaim deed. The $2,000 is added to the cost basis of the property.

3. **Tax Advice.** Section 212(3) allows the taxpayer to deduct expenses incurred in determining or resisting, or claiming the refund of, any tax liability (income, estate, or gift tax). Thus, legal fees paid in determining the tax consequences of a divorce or property settlement may be deducted by the taxpayer. [*See* Carpenter v. United States, 338 F.2d 366 (Ct. Cl. 1964)]

H. EXPENSES OF EDUCATION

1. **General Rule.** Educational costs which either qualify the taxpayer for a new trade or business, or which constitute the minimum educational requirement for qualification for his job, are never deductible.

2. **Deductible Educational Costs.** As long as they do not fall under the general rule above, the following expenses can be deducted:

    a. Education expenses that meet the express requirements of the individual's employer, or the requirements of law, as a condition to *retention* of a job or an increase in the rate of compensation.

    b. Education that *maintains* or *improves* skills required by the individual in his job or other trade or business.

3. **Qualified Educational Expenses--**

Carroll v. Commissioner, 418 F.2d 91 (7th Cir. 1969).

Facts. Carroll (P) was a Chicago police department detective who was taking undergraduate courses in preparation for law school. P was able to take classes since the Chicago police department instituted a program adjusting officers' work schedules to allow for continued education. P deducted $721 on his tax return for the cost of his enrollment at DePaul University. He justified the deduction under section 162(a) as an expense "relative to improving job skills to maintain his position as a detective." The Tax Court agreed with the Commissioner (D) that P had failed to demonstrate a sufficient relationship between his education and the particular job skills required as a police detective. P appeals.

Issue. Are college courses preparatory to law school sufficiently related to improving job skills as a police detective?

Held. No. Judgment affirmed.

- P might be allowed to deduct the cost of college courses which directly relate to the duties of his employment as a police detective. If such courses were taken along with other, more general courses, their cost, or that part of the tuition representing their cost, would be deductible under section 162(a).

- In this case, however, the courses of English, philosophy, history, and political science do not bear any greater relationship to P's job skills than general education.

I. PUBLIC POLICY

1. **Legal Expenses.** In *Commissioner v. Tellier,* 383 U.S. 687 (1966), a securities underwriter incurred legal expenses of almost $23,000 in unsuccessfully defending against charges of various securities violations and conspiracy. The Supreme Court allowed the deduction since the criminal charges were directly related to his business as an underwriter. Thus, the expenses were "ordinary and necessary" to the protection of his business. The Commissioner's contention that allowing such a deduction was contrary to public policy was rejected since no public policy is offended by a person defending against a criminal prosecution.

2. **Fines and Penalties.** Section 162(f) disallows a deduction for the payment of any fine or penalty to the government for the violation of any law. This includes penalties imposed under civil statutes as well as criminal statutes if the purpose is the same as would be accomplished under a criminal statute.

3. **Bribes and Kickbacks.** No deduction is allowed for any bribe, kickback, or payment to a government official or employee. Bribes and kickbacks to those outside of the government are also not deductible if their illegality can be established by criminal law or by a statute which subjects the violator to loss of a license or privilege of doing business. Also, as to the latter category, the IRS must show that the law that was violated is generally enforced. [I.R.C. §162(c)]

4. **Lobbying Activities.** Lobbying expenses incurred to influence any legislative body on a matter which is of direct interest to the taxpayer may be deducted as business expenses. [*See* I.R.C. §162(e)] A deduction is also allowed for that portion of membership dues paid to an organization attributable to that organization's expense in carrying on lobbying activities. Expenses of participating in political campaigns or influencing the general public are not deductible.

5. **Political Activities.** Except as provided in section 218, political campaign contributions are not deductible. Neither may a taxpayer claim a bad debt deduction for money that, loaned to a political party, becomes uncollectible.

VI. DEDUCTIONS FOR THE COSTS OF EARNING INCOME

A. CURRENT EXPENSES VERSUS CAPITAL EXPENDITURES

1. **Introduction.** The expenditure must be for business purposes rather than personal, and it must be ordinary and necessary. In addition, to be currently deductible, the expenditure must be an "expense" and not a "capital" expenditure. The question here is whether an expenditure can be deducted in the year made or must be "capitalized," which means that it is looked upon as the purchase of a business asset that will benefit the business for many future periods. This determination affects *when* the expenditure can be deducted. If an expenditure is capitalized, it can either be deducted over a period of years (as depreciation or amortization) *or* the capitalization will reduce the amount of gain recognized when the asset is finally sold (since all capital is first returned—as basis—before any net gain is taxed). Another important consideration is that capitalized items affect the amount of capital gain vis-a-vis ordinary income that is recognized. This will be discussed later in the outline.

2. **The Tax Impact of Capitalization.** When a taxpayer is permitted to deduct expenses currently that are incurred to produce income over subsequent years, the effect is that of tax deferral. In other words, the tax benefit (the deduction as an expense) is recognized immediately, while the income to which that benefit relates need not be claimed until it is earned in subsequent years. This deferral is not unlike the government granting the taxpayer an interest-free loan in the amount of the tax deferral. This is the reason behind the IRS's insistence that an expense that brings benefits to the taxpayer lasting over one year should be capitalized and then deducted periodically in future years as the benefits accrue to the taxpayer. Capitalization is also encouraged to avoid allowing the taxpayer to deduct an expense from ordinary income when the benefit will be taxed at capital gain rates. [*See* I.R.C. §263]

3. **Prepaid Expenses.**

   a. **Introduction.** A taxpayer is usually entitled to deduct expense items in the year in which they are paid. However, this generally does not apply to prepayments for goods and services to be received in future years. To allow deduction of prepaid expenses would permit a taxpayer to distort income by making voluntary prepayments to reduce taxes in years of high income. Note that disallowing prepayments does not do away with the deduction; rather, it forces the taxpayer to spread the expense over the same year in which the paid-for benefit is received.

b.   Advance payments--

Encyclopaedia Britannica v. Commissioner, 685 F.2d 212 (7th Cir. 1982).

Facts. Britannica (P) hired the David-Stewart Publishing Co. to prepare, edit, and arrange a manuscript to be later titled "The Dictionary of Natural Sciences." In return for receiving the complete manuscript, P was to pay advances against royalties expected to be earned from the book. P treated these advances as ordinary and necessary business expenses deductible in the years in which they were paid. This was done although no royalties had yet been received. The Commissioner (D) disallowed the deductions. The Tax Court held for P, stating that the expenditures were for "services" rather than for the acquisition of an asset. D appeals.

Issue. Are advances paid for a completed manuscript currently deductible even though the manuscript will produce future revenue?

Held. No. Judgment reversed and case remanded.

- The manuscript was intended to yield to P income over a period of years. The object of sections 162 and 263 is to match expenditures with the income they generate. Where the income is generated over a period of years, the expenditures should be capitalized and matched to revenues when they are produced.

- From the publisher's standpoint, a book is just another rental property. Just as the expenditures incurred in constructing a building must be capitalized, likewise, the expenditures incurred to create a book should be capitalized.

- P's argument that David-Stewart did nothing but render consulting services to P is erroneous. What P was buying was indeed a product (a completed manuscript). This was a "turnkey" project, remote from what is ordinarily understood to be editorial consultation.

Comments.

- The Seventh Circuit distinguished this case from the leading case of *Faura v. Commissioner*, 73 T.C. 849 (1980), where manuscript authors were allowed to deduct immediately expenses incurred in writing. The court noted that in *Faura*, the Tax Court only considered whether the author's expenditures were deductible at all and not whether, if they were deductible, they must first be capitalized.

- The 1986 Tax Act adopted I.R.C. section 263A, the Uniform Capitalization ("UNICAP") rules. The UNICAP rules provide extensive guidelines for the capitalization of all costs involved in the production of all self-created assets. These rules add a new layer of complexity to the income tax arena.

B. REPAIR AND MAINTENANCE EXPENSES

1. **Improvements and Repairs.** Expenditures which substantially prolong the life of an asset or increase its value should be capitalized. What is the treatment of costs which have characteristics both of deductible expenses and capital expenditures? Treasury Regulation sections 1.167(a) - 11(d)(2)(i) allow the taxpayer to deduct certain percentages of these expenses which are based on the cost of the asset. The percentage which is allowed varies with the nature of the asset and is set (rather arbitrarily) by the IRS.

2. **Start-Up Costs.** To be deductible as a business expense, the expense must have been incurred in "carrying on a trade or business." In *Richmond Television Corp. v. United States*, 345 F.2d 901 (4th Cir. 1965), a taxpayer was not allowed to deduct the expenses incurred in training broadcasters before he had an FCC license to broadcast. The court reasoned that the taxpayer was not a going concern performing business activities when the expenses were incurred.

3. **Experimental Costs.** I.R.C. section 174 allows a taxpayer to deduct "experimental expenditures which are paid or incurred by him during the taxable year in connection with his trade or business as expenses which are not chargeable to the capital account." This provision was enacted to stimulate the search for new products and ideas. The courts usually have allowed the deduction of these costs even before a business is being carried on or sales have begun. Also, section 174 allows the current deduction of research and experimental costs in creating patents, copyrights, etc., even though the benefits of such costs will stretch over future tax years (and would ordinarily be capital expenditures).

4. **Repairs vs. Improvements--**

Midland Empire Packing Co. v. Commissioner, 17 T.C. 635 (1950).

Facts. Midland (P) had been using the basement of its plant for curing meats for the past 25 years when it was discovered that oil was seeping into the area. P oilproofed the basement and deducted these costs as ordinary business expenses. The Commissioner (D) disallowed the deduction, claiming it to be a capital improvement adding to the depreciable basis of the building. P filed suit for a refund.

Issue. Should a building improvement which does not add to the useful life or value of the building be capitalized?

Held. No. Judgment for P.

♦   When an expenditure adds nothing of value to an asset but merely maintains it, then it is an ordinary and necessary business expense. Here P's oilproofing the basement kept the property in operating condition but did not add to its life.

Comment. Section 263(a)(1) provides that deductions may not be taken for amounts "paid out for new buildings or for permanent improvements or betterments made to increase the value of any property." Some of the criteria distinguishing capitalizations from expenses are:

(i)   Whether the expenditure prolongs the life of the property;

(ii)   Whether the improvements will endure over and beyond the taxable year;

(iii) Whether the expenditure adds to the value of the property;

(iv)   Whether the expenditure was part of an overall improvement or only a replacement of minor or recurring items; and

(v)   Whether there is a change or alteration in use or function.

---

5.   **Soil Remediation Costs--**

Revenue Ruling 94-38, 1994-1 C.B. 35.

Facts. X built a plant on land that was not contaminated. X's manufacturing operations discharge hazardous waste, which X buried on portions of its land. In 1993, in order to comply with environmental requirements, X decided to remediate the soil and groundwater that had been contaminated and to establish a system to monitor groundwater to avoid future environmental problems. X also constructed groundwater treatment facilities.

Issue. Are the groundwater remediation costs currently deductible as ordinary and necessary business expenses under section 162?

Answer. Yes. These costs are appropriate and helpful in carrying on X's business and are commonly and frequently required in X's type of business. The remediation project returned the property to its condition and value prior to the contamination. However, the costs of constructing the groundwater treatment facilities must be capitalized and depreciated over the tax life of the property since a new asset with a life greater than one year was created.

---

6.   **General Plan of Rehabilitation--**

Norwest Corporation and Subsidiaries v. Commissioner, 108 T.C. 265 (1977).

Facts. The taxpayer (P) built a building with asbestos-containing materials. P decided to remove the asbestos from the building in coordination with an overall remodeling project and deducted the cost of removal under IRC section 162. The Commissioner (D) disallowed the asbestos deduction, claiming that the costs must be capitalized pursuant to IRC section 263 or as part of a general plan of rehabilitation. Section 263 requires capitalization of costs incurred for permanent improvements, betterments, or restorations to property. P claims that the asbestos removal constitutes a repair since the removal did not increase the building's value when compared to its value before it was known to contain a hazardous material.

Issue. Is the removal cost of asbestos as part of a remodeling project a capital expenditure?

Held. Yes.

♦   The asbestos removal was part of one intertwined project, entailing a full-blown general plan of rehabilitation. The asbestos removal was done to effectuate the remodeling of the building. As costs associated with a general plan of rehabilitation and renovation increasing the value of the building, these costs must be capitalized.

C. INVENTORY ACCOUNTING

1. **Introduction.** When a manufacturer or retailer sells goods, the amount received is readily ascertainable. However, this amount is not gross income, since the cost of the goods sold must be subtracted from the gross receipts before gross income is attained. In some cases, it is possible to specifically tell the cost of each item sold. For example, a car dealer has little difficulty in keeping track of the costs of each automobile he sells. However, most manufacturers and retailers cannot possibly keep track of the costs of numerous items they sell. The method which was developed for dealing with this problem is through the use of inventories.

2. **The Inventory Concept.** The cost of goods sold is made up of (i) the goods on hand at the beginning of the year, *plus* (ii) goods purchased during the year, *minus* (iii) the goods on hand at the end of each year. The difficulty exists in valuating the units in the inventory at any given time, because the costs of each batch of inventory purchased may vary from other batches bought at other times, and there is difficulty in determining which batch is sold at what times (and hence there is difficulty in valuating or determining the cost of the goods sold and the cost of the goods remaining in inventory). This is particularly true during inflationary periods (since the price of units purchased is constantly going up). Were the goods sold during the year on hand at the beginning of the year, or were they acquired at higher prices later in the year?

3. **Inventory Valuation Methods.** The IRS allows a taxpayer to compute his inventory by one of a few accepted methods.

   a. **First in, first out.** If the "FIFO" method of inventory valuation is adopted, the taxpayer *assumes* that the goods first acquired were those which were first sold. The year-end inventory count is assumed to be made up of the goods last acquired. This method tends to show large profits in inflationary times since the cost of goods sold (which is deducted from gross receipts to arrive at gross income) consists of the lower-priced goods first acquired.

   b. **Last in, first out.** Under the "LIFO" method, the last goods acquired are assumed to have been sold first. The year-end inventory is thought to be made up of items which were first acquired. In a period of rising prices, this means that the cost of goods sold is increased, since the items sold were presumed to have been purchased later in the year. This, in turn, gives the taxpayer a larger deduction from gross receipts than the FIFO system would, so that his gross income is smaller. I.R.C. section 472 authorizes the use of the LIFO method, with its reduction in reported taxable income. However, section 472(c) requires that if a taxpayer uses LIFO for tax purposes, he must also use it for reporting to creditors and shareholders. Many entities are more concerned with showing a strong financial picture than in the tax savings offered by use of LIFO and hence they do not use the LIFO method.

4. **Indirect Costs.** For most retailers, the FIFO or LIFO method is adequate for determining the cost of goods sold. Manufacturers, however, must allocate various production costs to inventory items to reach a proper valuation figure. Cost of labor, materials, and overhead should be allocated to the various inventory items. However, taxpayers generally attempt to deduct "indirect" costs such as utilities and repairs as ordinary and necessary business expenses under I.R.C. section 162 rather than allocate such costs to inventory. For a long time, the Commissioner enjoyed success in the courts in requiring allocation of these costs. Finally, Treas. Reg. section 1.471-11 was adopted, which explicitly requires indirect costs to be allocated to inventories rather than be deducted directly under section 162. The Tax Reform Act of 1986 requires taxpayers to adopt the Uniform Capitalization Method for inventory accounting. Under this method, retailers and wholesalers are required to capitalize many types of indirect costs that they are currently deducting.

D. RENT PAYMENT VERSUS INSTALLMENT PURCHASE

1. **Common Law Foundation--**

Starr's Estate v. Commissioner, 274 F.2d 294 (9th Cir. 1959).

Facts. Starr (P) had a fire sprinkler system installed in his business. By the terms of the contract, P had a five-year lease of the system for $1,240 per year and an option to renew for an additional five years at $32 per year. P deducted $6,200 as rental expense. The Tax Court sustained the Commissioner's (D's) position that the $6,200 paid was a capital expenditure and not deductible as rental. Depreciation expense of $270 per year was allowed. P appeals.

Issue. Is a lease which provides for a renewal of the lease with nominal payments equivalent to a sale for tax purposes?

Held. Yes. Judgment affirmed in part; reversed in part.

♦   To distinguish a lease from a sale, form can be disregarded in favor of substance. In this case the sprinkler system was tailor-made for P's building, and it seems highly unlikely that it would be repossessed for its negligible salvage value. It is obvious that nominal rental payments of $32 after the lease renewal were nothing more than a service charge. It should be noted that the sprinkler company has never reclaimed a system at the end of the lease term. This transaction was a sale.

---

2.   **IRS Guidelines.** Rev. Rul. 75-21 sets forth guidelines for determining whether a transaction purported to be a lease will be treated as a lease for income tax purposes. A true lease will have the following characteristics:

   a.   The lessor will maintain an investment in the property throughout the life of the lease of at least 20% of the property's cost.

   b.   Any lease renewals must be at fair market value at the time of the renewal option.

   c.   The lessee may not have a contractual right to purchase the property at below fair market value.

   d.   A lessee may not furnish part of the leased property's cost nor improvements to be retained by the lessor.

   e.   No lessee may loan the lessor funds to purchase lease property.

   f.   The lessor must show that there is a reasonable expectation of profit from the lease.

E.   "ORDINARY AND NECESSARY"

1.   **Definition of "Ordinary and Necessary."** In *Commissioner v. Tellier*, 383 U.S. 687 (1966), the Court stated, "Our decisions have consistently con-

strued the term 'necessary' as imposing only the minimal requirement that the expense be 'appropriate and helpful' for 'the development of the taxpayer's business . . . .' The principal function of the term 'ordinary' . . . is to clarify the distinction, often difficult, between those expenses that are currently deductible and those that are in the nature of capital expenditures, which, if deductible at all, must be amortized over the useful life of the asset."

2. Payments for "Goodwill"--

Welch v. Helvering, 290 U.S. 111 (1933).

Facts. Welch (P) was the secretary of a grain company that was adjudged bankrupt and discharged from its debts. To aid in his relations with customers and solidify his own credit standing, P paid some of the debts of his former employer. The Commissioner (D) ruled that these were not ordinary and necessary business expenses, but were rather in the nature of capital outlays for development of goodwill. The Board of Tax Appeals and the court of appeals both affirmed. P appeals.

Issue. Are payments by a taxpayer to the creditors of his bankrupt former employer deductible if they were made to strengthen his own credit and personal reputation?

Held. No. Judgment affirmed.

♦   Ordinary and necessary business expenses are defined according to the normal means of conduct and forms of speech in the business world. Paying another's debts does not fall within this definition.

♦   Paying debts without legal obligation by the usage of trade is extraordinary, even if done for the purpose of strengthening one's credit. This is not the normal method of dealing with this type of business situation (*i.e.*, it is not an ordinary expense of doing business).

Comment. A taxpayer's payment of another's expenses or debts is not deductible unless the purpose of making the payment is to directly further or promote his own business.

3. Extraordinary Behavior--

Gilliam v. Commissioner, 51 T.C.M. 515 (1986).

Facts. Gilliam (P) was a noted artist who suffered from emotional disorders. P traveled frequently to lecture and teach. P was scheduled to make a trip to Memphis and was under a great deal of stress. Consequently, he contacted his doctor, who prescribed a new drug that P had never taken. P took the new medication before departing on the airplane to Memphis. Once airborne, P began to display irrational behavior. He began to attack a passenger and was arrested when the plane landed. P was found to be not guilty for his actions by reason of temporary insanity. P paid $9,250 and $9,600 for legal fees during 1975 and 1976. In addition, P paid the passenger that he attacked $3,900 in settlement of a civil claim. P deducted these amounts in 1975 and 1976. The Commissioner (D) disallowed the deductions.

Issue. Are the amounts paid by P ordinary and necessary business expenses?

Held. No. Judgment for D.

♦ The payments of expenses were for actions that were not directly connected with the taxpayer's trade or business. It is true that P was traveling on business, but his actions had no relationship to such business.

♦ The payments were not ordinary for the type of business that P was conducting.

Comments.

♦ In *Dancer v. Commissioner,* 73 T.C. 1103 (1980), the taxpayer was allowed a deduction for expenses of litigation arising out of an accident occurring on a business trip. However, in *Dancer,* the taxpayer's actions were ordinary and were related to his trade or business.

♦ In *Friedman v. Delaney*, 171 F.2d 269 (1st Cir. 1948), an attorney paid the debt his client owed to creditors and then tried to deduct it as a bad business debt. The court denied the deduction, noting that his profession in no way required P to voluntarily pay a client's debts. As such this was a personal rather than business obligation and hence not deductible for income tax purposes.

---

4. **Reasonable Compensation.**

   a. **Introduction.** Section 162(a)(1) allows a taxpayer to deduct a "reasonable allowance for salaries or other compensation for personal services actually rendered." Reasonable compensation is determined by all relevant facts and circumstances.

   b. **Salary based on profits.** A salary based on a percentage of income or profits is deductible even if unreasonable (in terms of the work performed for the amount of compensation received) if it is found that a "free bargain" was entered into in setting the compensation amount. In *Harold's Club v. Commissioner,* 340 F.2d 861 (9th Cir. 1965), the two owners of a casino paid to their father, who founded and managed the club, a base salary plus 20% of the profits of the club. The court found that a free bargain did not exist because the casino owners were dominated by their father. The taxpayer argued that it should make no difference if a business deducts large salaries as long as the recipient claims the income and pays taxes on it.

c. **Golden parachute payments.** I.R.C. section 280G restricts deductions for substantial bonuses paid to corporate executives contingent on the change in control of the company. The amount disallowed is based on a formula that factors in the taxpayer's average compensation for a five-year period.

d. **Compensation to shareholder-employees.** Corporations frequently attempt to deduct as business expenses large salaries paid to executives who are also shareholders of the corporation. The IRS tries to get these salaries classified as nondeductible (to the corporation) dividends. Salary payments that have no relationship to the value of the services rendered are therefore not deductible as ordinary business expenses.

5. **Costs of Illegal or Unethical Activities.**

a. **The basic rule.** Section 162 expenses and losses that would otherwise be deductible are not if to do so would violate public policy.

b. **Pre-1970 case law development.** Prior to 1970, several Supreme Court decisions attempted to delineate which seemingly allowable deductions violated public policy. This led to much discontent as the decisions were viewed as inconsistent. The Court disallowed the deduction of fines paid for violating state trucking laws [Tank Truck Rentals v. Commissioner, 356 U.S. 30 (1958)] but allowed deductions for rent and wages that an illegal state bookmaking operation paid [Commissioner v. Sullivan, 356 U.S. 27 (1958)]. In *Commissioner v. Tellier,* 383 U.S. 687 (1966), the court allowed a securities dealer convicted of securities and mail fraud violations to deduct his legal fees in defending himself. These and other decisions led to congressional amendments to section 162, effective in 1970.

c. **Fines and penalties.** In 1969, Congress added subsection (f) to section 162. This subsection disallows a deduction for the payment of any fine or penalty to the government for the violation of any law. This includes penalties imposed under civil statutes as well as criminal statutes if the purpose is the same as would be accomplished under a criminal statute.

d. **Bribes and kickbacks.** Congress further added subsection (c) to section 162. It states that no deduction is allowed for any bribe, kickback, or payment to a government official or employee. Bribes and kickbacks to those outside of the government are also not deductible if their illegality can be established by criminal law or by a statute which subjects the violator to the loss of a license or privilege of doing business. Also, as to the latter category, the IRS must show that the law that was violated is generally enforced.

e.   **Restitution payment--**

Stephens v. Commissioner, 905 F.2d 667 (2d Cir. 1990).

Facts. Stephens (P) was convicted of four counts of wire fraud, one count of fraud in interstate commerce, and one count of conspiracy for defrauding Raytheon, a Delaware corporation. P was sentenced to a five-year concurrent prison term and a $1,000 fine for each count of wire fraud. P was sentenced to a five-year term and a $5,000 fine for the other count of fraud. The last five-year term was suspended on the condition that P make restitution to Raytheon in the amount of $1 million ($530,000 representing the principal that P had embezzled and $470,000 representing interest). P paid taxes on the $530,000 when he received it in 1976. In 1984, P paid Raytheon the $530,000 and executed a $470,000 promissory note. P deducted the $530,000 on an amended 1984 tax return. The Commissioner (D) disallowed the deduction and the Tax Court found for D. P appeals.

Issue. May a taxpayer claim as a deduction a restitution payment of embezzled funds?

Held. Yes. Judgment reversed.

♦   A taxpayer is allowed to deduct an uncompensated loss incurred in a transaction entered into for profit, even though it is not connected with a trade or business. [I.R.C. §165(c)(2)] However, case law prohibits deductions under section 165 where the allowance would severely and immediately frustrate national or state policies proscribing particular types of conduct. Ordinarily, taxpayers who repay embezzled funds are entitled to a deduction in the year in which the funds are repaid. D argues that P's deduction should be disallowed because the payment was made in lieu of punishment; to allow the deduction would take the "sting" out of Ps punishment, thereby frustrating public policy. We hold that because P already paid taxes on the embezzled funds, disallowing the deduction for repaying the funds would result in a "double sting." In addition, P was given a stern sentence of five years in prison and fined $16,000. Thus, allowing the deduction would not frustrate public policy.

♦   We also consider the codification of the public policy exception in section 162, with regard to the deductibility of business expenses. Section 162 limits the exception to illegal payments such as bribes and kickbacks, fines or penalties paid to the government, and a portion of treble damage payments under antitrust laws. Although the public policy exception to deductibility of losses under section 165 was not explicitly affected by the amendments to section 162, we believe that Congress could not have intended to prohibit certain deductions under section 162 but allow them under section 165. Here, P's payment was not a fine or penalty because it was compensatory rather than punitive in nature. Also, P made its payment to Raytheon, not to the government. Thus, the exception for fines or penalties paid to the government in section 162 does not preclude deduction of P's restitution payment.

————————

F. DEPRECIATION

1. **Introduction.** I.R.C. section 167 permits as a depreciation deduction a "reasonable allowance for the exhaustion, wear, and tear" of assets used in a trade or business *or* held for the production of income. All physical property used in a trade or business or for the production of income may be depreciated if it has a limited useful life. Also, intangible assets (copyrights, etc.) may be depreciated unless their useful life is indefinite.

2. **Pre-1981 Depreciation.** Prior to the Economic Recovery Tax Act of 1981 (ERTA), depreciation was computed by taking the cost of an asset (less salvage value) and allocating it over the useful life of the asset by an accepted depreciation method.

   a. **Useful life.** The ADR (asset depreciation range) system (I.R.C. section 167(m)) listed broad classes of assets with estimated useful lives published by the IRS. A taxpayer could elect a useful life within 20% of these guidelines without IRS challenge. If the taxpayer used a useful life outside of this range, then he had the burden of showing the reasonableness of the estimation.

   b. **Methods.** Any "reasonable" method for allocating the cost of the wasting asset over its useful life was acceptable, but could not result in a faster write-off than that allowed by the "double declining-balance method." The most common depreciation methods are "straight-line," "sum-of-the-years-digits," and "declining-balance" methods.

3. **Post-1980 Depreciation.** ERTA made vast changes to the long-held depreciation concepts previously used under common law and ADR.

   a. **Personal property.** There are now six different classes of property. Each of these classes reference old ADR lives and include the following personal property: Three-year (special tools and racehorses); five-year (automobiles, computers, copiers, semiconductor manufacturing equipment, typewriters, etc.); seven-year (office furniture, fixtures, and equipment, agricultural single purpose buildings, etc.); 10-year (petroleum refining assets); 15-year (sewage treatment and telephone distribution plants); and 20-year (municipal sewers). Taxpayers can elect to use longer lives for the assets.

The method prescribed for personal property is 200% declining balance for three-year, five-year, seven-year, and 10-year categories. The method prescribed for 15-year and 20-year personal property is 150% declining balance. However, taxpayers can elect to use the straight-line method to postpone deductions. In addition, a half-year convention is used for the year the property is placed in service. Only a half-year's deduction is allowed in the year the property is sold.

b. **Useful lives of real property.** Real property is depreciated (or recovered) under ACRS. The recovery periods for real estate are 27.5 years for residential rental property and 31.5 years for other property.

c. **Expensing.** I.R.C. section 179 allows taxpayers to expense up to $10,000 per year. The expensing rules are only applicable to the cost of personal property.

4. **Computation.**

a. **Straight-line.** Under this method, the cost of the property, less salvage value, is divided by the useful life of the property. Suppose that a taxpayer purchases, for $12,500, a machine which has a useful life of six years and a salvage value of $500. Each year he could claim depreciation of $2,000 (*i.e.*, ($12,500 - $500)/6).

b. **Declining-balance methods.** Here each year's depreciation is computed by subtracting from the property's basis the amount already written off, and applying a constant rate to the remaining basis. For example, if a taxpayer purchases a machine for $10,500 with a useful life of five years and a salvage value of $500, depreciation computed under the 150% declining-balance method would be as follows:

Year	Rate	Year's Depreciation	Remaining Basis
			$10,500
1	150%	$3,150	7,350
2	150%	2,205	5,145
3	150%	1,543	3,602
4	150%	1,081	2,521
5	remainder	2,521	-0-

5. **Disposition of Depreciable Property.** Much of the property eligible for I.R.C. section 1231 (or capital gain) treatment is also property that can be depreciated under section 167. Thus, a taxpayer could take ordinary depreciation deductions and then claim a capital gain upon disposition of the property. Sections 1245 and 1250 were enacted to eliminate this taxpayer practice, which had the effect of converting ordinary income into capital gain. These

sections require a taxpayer to report certain portions of section 1231 gain as ordinary income.

a. **Section 1245.** This section requires that upon the sale of depreciable personal property, any gain realized is ordinary income to the extent of all depreciation deductions taken after 1963. For example, taxpayer bought a machine in 1970 for $20,000 and deducted $12,000 depreciation from 1970 to 1979. In 1979, taxpayer sold the machine for $23,000; the gain realized is $15,000. Section 1245 requires that $12,000 of this gain be recognized as ordinary income. The remaining $3,000 receives favorable capital gain treatment.

b. **Section 1250.**

   1) **Introduction.** This section requires that "additional" depreciation claimed on buildings be recaptured. This means any depreciation in excess of the straight-line rate. For example, suppose that a taxpayer purchased a residential building in 1970 for $100,000. The building had an expected useful life of 50 years. When the building was sold in 1980, depreciation of $32,000 had been claimed. Of this, the straight-line amount was $20,000. If the building was sold for $85,000, the gain realized would be $17,000 since the basis at that date was $68,000. Section 1250 requires that $12,000 of the $17,000 gain be recognized as ordinary income, since that amount represents accelerated depreciation over the straight-line rate. Section 1250(a)(1)(B) relaxes the recapture rule for owners of housing units for low-income renters. If such buildings are held for over 100 months, the amount of the recapture is decreased by 1% for each month held over 100 months. Therefore, if a low-income housing unit were held for 120 months before being sold, 20% of the normally recaptured accelerated depreciation would be forgiven and the gain recognized to that extent would be capital gain.

   2) **ERTA qualification.** ERTA leaves the law unchanged for residential real property. However, it requires the entire amount of prior depreciation to be recaptured as ordinary income if accelerated depreciation was used for nonresidential real property.

6. **Nondepreciables.** To be depreciable, an asset must have a limited useful life. Thus, land or stocks cannot be depreciated. Intangible assets that have limited useful lives must be depreciated (or amortized) over statutory lives.

7. **Basis for Depreciating Debt-Financed Property.**

a. **General rule.** The amount of debt incurred in financing a depreciable asset is included in the property's basis for purposes of computing depreciation. This is the "basis" side of the *Crane* holding, *supra*.

b. **Limitation—non-real estate investments.** I.R.C. section 465 states that depreciation and other deductions cannot exceed the taxpayer's actual investment or liability in the investment. These are known as the "at risk" limitations and apply to all investments other than real estate. The Tax Reform Act of 1986 extended the "at risk" rule to certain real estate investments.

G. DEPLETION

1. **Introduction.** I.R.C. section 611 allows the owner of a wasting asset (oil, gas, minerals, gravel, timber, etc.) to deduct a reasonable allowance for its use or exploitation. A wasting asset is any deposit which is consumed by use or exploitation. There are two methods of computing depletion.

   a. **Cost method.** The cost of the wasting asset is divided by the estimated number of units recoverable to obtain a cost per unit. This figure is the deduction that may be claimed for each unit which is extracted. For example, if the total cost of drilling an oil well is $30 million and it is estimated that five million barrels of oil will be recovered from the well, the owner could claim $6 depletion for each barrel of oil which is ultimately recovered.

   b. **Percentage method.** In the percentage method, a fixed percentage must be used, depending on the type of wasting asset involved. The percentage is taken from gross income to arrive at the deduction. Congress sets the percentage figure, which ranges from 5% of receipts for gravel to 22% for sulfur and uranium. This method has the advantage of continued life, in contrast with cost depletion, which runs out when the cost of the asset is fully recovered.

   c. **Intangible drilling costs.** Intangible drilling costs are costs incurred in the drilling of a well. The taxpayer has the option of either deducting these costs or capitalizing them and then claiming depletion on their costs. [*See* I.R.C. §263(c)] The most advantageous method would be to deduct the costs and then use the percentage depletion method, which is a percentage of gross income, not of cost.

H. TAX AVOIDANCE AND TAX SHELTERS

1. **Introduction.** A growing number of investments are called tax shelters because they shelter an investor's other income from tax. This is accomplished in one or more of three ways.

   a. **Deferral.** A tax shelter investment usually generates substantial tax losses in the early years of the investment. The deductions producing these losses are often produced through depreciation and require no out-of-pocket outlay. Taxable income, if any, is produced in later years of the investment's life. The effect is to defer payment of tax until the later, non-loss years.

b. **Leverage.** This is the use of someone else's money to finance an investment. Leverage allows a taxpayer (through the *Crane* rule) to increase the depreciable basis to include external financing. In abusive shelters, a nonrecourse loan is made and included in the taxpayer's basis. This allows the taxpayer to claim inflated deductions, such as depreciation, without risking his own capital.

c. **Conversion.** This means the conversion of ordinary income to capital gain. For example, if accelerated depreciation is taken against property, it reduces ordinary income. Later, when the property is sold, the increased gain realized from the lower basis is given capital gain treatment. Various recapture provisions have limited the usefulness of this strategy.

2. **Use of Limited Partnerships.** The most common business form for sheltering income is the partnership. In contrast to corporations, a partnership allows investors direct flow-through of depreciation and other deductions as well as investment tax credits. The investor also uses this form to limit his liability while increasing his investment basis through the use of nonrecourse loans (thus increasing tax deductions such as depreciation).

3. **Tax Shelters as Investments.** Tax shelters should provide an economic rate of return like any other investment. However, many taxpayers are too concerned with tax savings to carefully examine the quality of the investment. Some tax shelters are characterized by overpriced assets, high syndication costs, and poor management. On the other hand, some tax shelters are sound investments. A good shelter has a strong economic base and tax benefits that increase the rate of return. In addition, investors should carefully read the tax opinions and offering materials. The offering materials are required to include a summary of facts, identification of material federal income tax issues, opinion on each such material issue, and an overall evaluation of the proposed tax benefits.

4. **Common Tax Shelters.**

a. **The motion picture tax shelter.** The motion picture industry attracts investment capital by sharing its tax benefits with the investors. The principal tax benefits are twofold: (i) an investor gets a tax deferment through large front-end deductions; and (ii) investors are able to borrow funds without personal liability and thereby obtain deductions in excess of their cash investments. Usually a limited partnership is used here so that losses are passed on to the investors without subjecting them to personal liability.

b. **Farming tax shelters.** Tax sheltering opportunities were granted by Congress to stimulate farming investment. Today, this shelter is used by high tax bracket nonfarming investors via limited partnerships. The sheltering opportunities in this area come in many different forms. Farmers are allowed an immediate deduction of development costs, rather than capitalizing and amortizing them. Also, a farmer or rancher is allowed to characterize the sales of some of his products as producing a capital gain.

c. **Oil and gas tax shelters.** Congress provides incentives for investment in exploration of oil and gas. Along with the advantage of leverage (deducting costs which were financed with another's money, sometimes through a nonrecourse loan), other attractions exist. An oil and gas investor is allowed an immediate deduction for intangible drilling costs. These comprise about 70% of mineral exploration costs. This, of course, gives the investor a tax deferment benefit. Also, if percentage depletion, *supra* H.1.b., is used by the taxpayer, he might have the opportunity to claim depletion in excess of the well's basis. However, these shelters are subject to continual revision. Starting in 1976, only small independent producers are allowed to use percentage depletion.

d. **Real estate tax shelters.** Real estate is the most extensively used tax shelter. Besides being a good tax shelter, real estate investments are generally a good inflation hedge. Probably the greatest tax advantage in this area is the ability to deduct depreciation, sometimes at accelerated rates. The two principal types of real estate investments are discussed below.

    1) **Land investments.** The greatest advantage in land investments is the ability to deduct interest and taxes even when a nominal down payment was made. Also, an investor may make a trade for other land or improved real estate tax-free. Finally, a sale of land is taxable at capital gains rates.

    2) **Improved real estate.** Along with the tax advantages discussed above, investments in land and buildings add the additional shelter of depreciation. This allows the taxpayer to deduct a portion of the building's cost to show the decline in the property's value. However, depreciation is allowed even in an inflationary economy, in which a building's value may increase, rather than decline.

5. **Legislative Response to Sheltering.** Congress and its Ways and Means Committee are continually groping to find an equitable way to treat the various tax shelters. The following are some laws which address this problem.

    a. **Depreciation recapture.** I.R.C. sections 1245 and 1250 are introduced in the capital gains chapter. The objective of these two sections is to convert a portion of a taxpayer's capital gain to ordinary income. Since deductions were taken at ordinary rates, these two sections eliminate some of the negative tax advantage inherent in most tax shelter investments.

b. **Investment interest deductions.** I.R.C. section 163(d) limits the amount of deductible interest to the amount of the taxpayer's net investment income. Net investment income includes net income from investment properties and gains from the sale of such properties. Interest, royalties, and dividends are no longer treated as investment income.

c. **Capitalization of costs.** I.R.C. section 263(a) requires taxpayers to capitalize many items that were formerly deductible in the current year. In addition, this section requires taxpayers to capitalize interest and taxes incurred during the construction of an asset.

d. **At-risk limitation.** I.R.C. section 465 provides that deductions cannot exceed the taxpayer's actual investment or liability in the investment. Therefore, nonrecourse debt is excluded from the taxpayer's "at-risk" basis in the investment. There are exceptions to these rules for certain real estate investments.

e. **Passive loss rules.** I.R.C. section 469 limits deductions from passive activities to income from such activities. A passive activity is one where the taxpayer does not "materially participate" in the conduct of the trade or business. All limited partnership interests are passive investments. In addition, property held for rent is defined to be passive. All of the taxpayer's passive activities are combined and tested for net passive income or loss. Passive losses can be carried forward indefinitely.

6. **Penalties Introduced by TEFRA.**

a. **Promoter penalties.** In an effort to attack abusive tax shelters at their source, Congress in 1982 authorized a penalty, equal to the greater of $1,000 or 10% of the gross income derived from a tax shelter activity, on promoters, organizers, or sellers who make statements that they know or have reason to know are false regarding the availability of tax benefits, or statements that "grossly overvalue" property or services. [I.R.C. §6700]

b. **Substantial underpayment of tax.** If a taxpayer has not disclosed a material matter or has taken a position that lacks substantial authority, then a tax equal to 10% of any "substantial underpayment" of tax is authorized under section 6661.

c. **Aiding and abetting.** TEFRA also added a penalty for aiding and abetting the understatement of tax liability under section 6701. This section also provides for injunctions against promoters of abusive tax shelters and added or increased other penalties.

7. **Tax Shelter Limitations Imposed by the Tax Reform Acts of 1984 and 1986.**

    a. **Contributed property allocations.** Previously, a partner's share of income, loss, deduction, and credit was determined according to the partnership agreement. Since the partner's basis for contributed property carried over to the partnership, any pre-contribution appreciation or depreciation in value was included in partnership income or loss on its disposition. The 1984 Act requires that partnerships specially allocate income and deductions to partners to reflect the difference between the adjusted basis of contributed property and its fair market value at contribution.

    b. **Prepaid expenses.** Previously, a cash basis taxpayer could currently deduct expense prepayments that related to the coming 12 months. These rules were exploited by prepaying the next year's expenses at year-end. Under the 1984 Act, tax shelters are not allowed a deduction until the amount is paid and economic performance occurs. Economic performance occurs when services are performed, property provided, use of property occurs, or liability is satisfied. Starting in 1987, tax shelters were required to use the accrual method of accounting.

    c. **Property distributions.** Generally, property contributions are tax-free and partnership cash distributions are likewise tax-free to the extent of the partner's basis in the partnership. The IRS would argue that a property contribution followed by an immediate cash distribution should give rise to immediate income. Under the 1984 Act, a contribution by a partner to a partnership followed by a related transfer to the partner is taxable if it is properly characterized as a sale.

    d. **Like-kind exchanges of partnership interests.** The IRS has long argued that partnership interests could not be exchanged tax-free. Several courts disagreed, looking to the underlying assets of the partnerships to determine if the exchange qualified for like-kind treatment. Under the 1984 Act, partnership interests do not qualify for like-kind exchange treatment.

8. **Registration Requirements Under 1984 Act.** Under the 1984 Act, anyone organizing an investment expected to generate specific levels of tax benefits and to meet investor criteria must register the shelter with the IRS and obtain a tax shelter I.D. number. This number must be furnished to all investors, who will then disclose it on their tax returns. Qualifying tax shelter investments are those expected to generate deductions in excess of twice any investor's cumulative investment at the end of the first five years of invest-

ment. If this two-to-one ratio is met, registration is required if the investment must be registered under federal or state securities laws, if it is exempt from filing, or if the aggregate amount that may be offered for sale to investors exceeds $250,000, with five or more investors expected.

9. **Promoter Lists.** The 1984 Act also required that persons who organize or sell interests in "potentially abusive tax shelters" must maintain lists identifying purchasers and other information.

10. **Administrative Response.** The IRS has issued numerous Revenue Rulings making a strict interpretation of the Code and Treasury Regulations.

   a. **At-risk limitations.** Rev. Rul. 77-397, 1977-2 C.B. 178, held that a sale of a master recording with a reversion to the seller after two years amounted to a lease. This invoked I.R.C. section 465, which limited the seller's losses from the shelter to his at-risk investment.

   b. **Basis limitations.** Rev. Rul. 77-110, 1977-1 C.B. 58, holds a nonrecourse note not includable in the investor's basis if the investor's liability is effectively contingent. Rev. Rul. 77-398, 1977-2 C.B. 179, excludes from the investor's basis a liability which is paid back only from the shelter's profits. Rev. Rul. 77-401, 1977-2 C.B. 215, excludes from a partner's basis an investment loan secured by a note with recourse only against the partnership.

   c. **Liability forgiveness.** Rev. Rul. 77-402, 1977-2 C.B. 222, requires a selling partner to include his share of liabilities reduced or forgiven through the sale to be included in the amount realized.

11. **Basic Judicial Doctrine.**

   a. **Interest.**

      1) **Is the obligation a bona fide debt?--**

Knetsch v. United States, 364 U.S. 361 (1960).

Facts. Knetsch (P) purchased 10 $400,000 deferred annuity savings bonds from a life insurance company bearing 2.5% interest. P paid for the bonds with $4,000 cash and a $4 million nonrecourse note at 3.5% interest. P was allowed to borrow the excess cash value of the bonds over his indebtedness before it became due each year. In 1954, P paid the first year's interest of $140,000 to the insurance company, then borrowed what was the increase in value over that year, $99,000, and then paid $3,465 interest on that. He then sought to deduct the full $143,465 as interest expenses. P followed the same process in 1955 and 1956. The Commissioner (D) disallowed the deductions and assessed P with a deficiency. P paid and brought suit in district court, which entered judgment for D, and the court of appeals affirmed. P appeals.

Issue. Was P's obligation to the insurance company a bona fide debt?

Held. No. Judgment affirmed.

♦　There was nothing of substance to be realized by P from his transaction beyond a tax deduction. What he was ostensibly "lent" back was in reality only a rebate of a substantial part of the so-called "interest" payments. The $91,570 difference retained by the insurance company was its fee for providing the facade of loans for P.

♦　This transaction was a sham, serving no economic interest of P's other than to reduce his taxes.

Dissent. No part of this transaction was a sham. Tax avoidance is a dominating purpose behind scores of transactions.

Comment. A transaction must affect the taxpayer's beneficial interest to raise an interest deduction. Interest is not deductible *unless* the taxpayer had some purpose other than (or along with) tax savings in incurring the debt. Today, section 163(d) limits investment interest deduction to net investment income.

---

2) **Tax-exempt interest**. Section 265(2) does not allow the deduction of interest paid on tax-exempt state or municipal bonds.

b. **The "at-risk" requirement.**

1) **Judicial background--**

Estate of Franklin v. Commissioner, 544 F.2d 1045 (9th Cir. 1976).

Facts. Charles T. Franklin was a limited partner in a partnership that made a "purchase" of a hotel from the Romneys. Under the agreement, the Romneys sold the property to the partnership for $1,224,000. The price was to be paid over 10 years except that a "prepayment" of interest of $75,000 was paid at the outset and a balloon payment of $975,000 was to be paid at the end of the 10-year period. The partnership had the deed placed in escrow but it was not recorded. The partnership leased the property back to the Romneys, with the lease payments equaling the mortgage payments. Thus, no additional cash changed hands between the two parties. The lease was a net lease, *i.e.*, the Romneys incurred all the expenses normally associated with property ownership. The Commissioner (D) ruled the transaction to be an option, and disallowed the partnership's deductions of interest and depreciation. The Tax Court ruled for D, and Franklin's estate (P) appeals.

Issue. If a taxpayer has no equity in a property due to the nature of an investment, can deductions such as interest still be taken?

Held. No. Judgment affirmed.

♦ This transaction more closely resembled an option than a purchase of realty. Due to the low property value, payments on the principal of the purchase price yielded no equity in the property since the purchase price exceeded the property's fair market value.

♦ Depreciation is predicated on an "investment" in property. No such investment exists here since payments of the purchase price yield no equity to the purchaser.

♦ The absence of personal liability on the debt reduces the transaction in economic terms to a mere chance that a genuine debt obligation may arise. Since there is not a bona fide debt, no interest deductions are allowed.

---

2) **Statutory refinement.** As previously noted, I.R.C. section 465 now states that depreciation and other deductions cannot exceed the taxpayer's actual investment or liability in the investment. These are known as the "at-risk" limitations and apply to all investments other than real estate.

12. **Corporate Tax Shelters.**

   a. **Consolidated tax returns.** If one corporation owns at least 80% of the stock of another, they can elect to file consolidated returns. [I.R.C. §§1501, 1504] Under this election, the corporations are treated for many purposes like a single corporation. For example, intercorporate sales of goods or services are not taxed, and losses of one corporation can be offset against gains of another.

   b. **Section 482.** Related corporations frequently deal with one another. Sometimes there are tax advantages in not having the corporations deal at arm's length. For example, if one corporation is domestic and the second is a foreign corporation in a country with a low tax rate, it would be advantageous for the American corporation to sell its goods at a low profit margin to the foreign corporation and have this corporation take the profit (at a lower tax rate). I.R.C. section 482 gives the IRS the power to reallocate items of income and/or deductions between businesses controlled directly or indirectly by the same interests.

   c. **Unreasonable accumulations of surplus—the accumulated earnings tax.**

1) **Introduction.** The accumulated earnings tax is aimed at corporations formed for the purpose of aiding its shareholders in avoiding tax by accumulating income rather than distributing taxable dividends to its shareholders. I.R.C. section 531 provides that a corporation is subject to the tax if it is "formed or availed for the purpose of avoiding the income tax with respect to its shareholders, by permitting its earnings and profits to accumulate instead of being distributed."

2) **The "reasonable needs" test.** If earnings and profits are accumulated by a corporation beyond its reasonable needs, I.R.C. section 533(a) imposes a tax on the excess. Reasonable needs include expansion, construction, or working capital requirements.

3) **Calculating the tax.** In addition to a reasonable needs deduction, a corporation is not taxed on the amount by which accumulated earnings at the beginning of the year are less than $250,000 (except for professional service corporations (law, medicine, etc.) which are taxed beginning at $150,000). [I.R.C. §535(c)(2)] The tax itself is computed on an annual basis on accumulated taxable income, with a 27.5% rate on the first $100,000, and a 38.5% rate on the excess.

d. **Personal holding companies.** Sections 541-547 impose a tax on undistributed income of personal holding companies. Personal holding companies are corporations that receive passive forms of income and are considered "pocketbooks" for their shareholders. The tax is not imposed unless over one-half of the company's stock is held by no more than five people.

e. **Life insurance policies--**

Winn-Dixie Stores, Inc. v. Commissioner, 254 F.3d 1313 (11th Cir. 2001), *cert. denied*, 535 U.S. 986 (2002).

Facts. Winn-Dixie (P) instituted a company-owned life insurance ("COLI") program that involved P's purchasing whole life insurance policies for tens of thousands of full-time employees. P was the sole beneficiary of the policies. Because P borrowed against the policies' account value at an interest rate of 11% and incurred administrative fees, P incurred costs greater than the net cash surrender value and benefits paid on the policies. P lost money on the program, but planned to benefit in the billions of dollars over 60 years as a result of post-tax deductibility of the interest and fees. In 1997, after a change in tax law jeopardized this tax arbitrage, P eased out of the program. As a result of interest and fee deductions taken in 1993, the Commissioner (D) determined a deficiency. P brought suit; the Tax Court found for D. P appeals.

Issue. Is P entitled to deduct interest and fees incurred in borrowing against insurance policies that it owned on the lives of more than 36,000 Winn-Dixie employees?

Held. No. Judgment affirmed.

♦ The special treatment Congress affords to life insurance contracts whose benefits are generally untaxed and whose appreciation is tax-deferred [*see* I.R.C. §§101(a)(1), 72(e)] extends to loans made against a policy, whose interest is generally not deductible. [*See* I.R.C. §§264(a)(3)] If no part of the annual premium is financed by a policy loan in four of the first seven years, the interest is deductible. Although P's loans fell within the exception, the sham-transaction doctrine applies here as it did in *Knetsch v. United States* (*supra*). As in *Knetsch*, which involved an annuity contract, the insurance program was being used as a tax shelter and offers P no financial benefit other than its tax consequences.

♦ The sham-transaction doctrine provides that a transaction is not entitled to tax respect if it lacks economic effects or substance other than the generation of tax benefits, or if the transaction serves no business purpose. The Tax Court was correct in concluding that the COLI program had no function other than generating interest deductions; it could never generate a pretax profit. This is probably the reason P eased out of the program after the 1996 tax law changes threatened the benefits that P was receiving under the program.

---

13. **The Alternative Minimum Tax.**

   a. **Introduction.** Once taxable income is calculated by reducing gross income and adjusted gross income by the deductions to which a taxpayer is entitled (including deductions arising from capital gains and losses), the percentage tax rates (I.R.C. section 1) are applied to determine the tax payable. However, an "alternative minimum tax" may apply. [I.R.C. §55]

   b. **A "minimum," not an "election."** The alternative minimum tax ("AMT") applies only if it results in a higher tax than otherwise computed using the tax tables or tax rate schedules. The objective of the AMT is to impose a minimum level of tax on taxpayers who shelter their regular tax liability by using preference items. The tax is based on a broader definition of income and is imposed at a 26% rate on the first $175,000 alternative minimum taxable income ("AMTI"), and at 28% on any additional AMTI.

   c. **Computation.** First compute AMTI. The term AMTI means regular taxable income determined with adjustments under I.R.C. sections 56 and 58 and increased by tax preference items described in I.R.C. section 57. Then subtract an exemption ($69,950 on a joint return, $46,200 for a single person, $34,975 for the single return of a married person). The exemption amounts are phased out when taxpayer's AMTI exceeds certain levels. The balance is taxable at the rate of 26% on the first $175,000 and 28% on the balance. The taxpayer then pays either his regular tax or the alternative minimum tax, whichever is the greater amount.

d. **Adjustments under I.R.C. section 56.** The adjustments required to compute AMTI are as follows:

1) Depreciation shall be computed under the straight-line method.

2) No deductions shall be allowed for any miscellaneous itemized deduction, taxes, or standard deduction.

3) The medical deduction will be limited to 10% of AGI floor rather than 7.5%.

4) Interest will be allowed only for loans to purchase or improve a personal residence plus one second residence and investment interest (not to exceed net investment income).

5) Mining exploration costs must be amortized over a 10-year period.

6) Long-term contracts must reflect the percentage of completion method of accounting.

7) Fifty percent of the excess of "book" income (*i.e.*, income reported on financial statements) over AMTI.

8) Others: the phase-in rules for passive losses and losses from farm tax shelters will not be allowed. [I.R.C. §58]

e. **Tax preferences.** The tax preferences subject to the AMT include:

1) Certain tax-exempt interest.

2) Financial institution bad debt reserves.

3) Pre-1987 ACRS deductions on leased personal property in excess of a figure computed using straight-line depreciation over a useful life of five years (for three-year property) and eight years (for five-year property).

4) Pre-1987 deductions on 15-year real property (whether or not leased) in excess of straight-line depreciation.

5) The bargain element of an incentive stock option when exercised.

6) The excess of percentage depletion over adjusted basis of a mine or oil and gas well.

7) The gain portion of charitable contributions of appreciated property.

8) Intangible drilling costs on oil and gas wells (less the amount of such costs that would be recovered through straight-line depreciation) in excess of net income from oil and gas.

f. **Credits.** A credit will be allowed to reduce regular tax for AMT paid attributable to timing items. Timing items are items that are included in AMTI currently but will be in regular taxable income in future years.

g. **Applies to taxpayers with no tax preferences--**

Klaasen v. Commissioner, 182 F.3d 932 (10th Cir. 1999) (unpublished opinion).

Facts. The Klaasens' (Ps') religious beliefs encouraged them to have a large family. In 1994, Ps rightfully claimed 12 exemptions, 10 for their children and two for themselves. Ps itemized their deductions, claiming $4,767.13 in medical deductions and $3,263.56 in state and local taxes. Ps did not complete the AMT form with their 1994 return. The Commissioner (D) sent a notice of deficiency for $1,085.43 in minimum taxes for 1994. Ps claimed that since they do not have any tax preference items within the meaning of section 57 they are not subject to minimum tax. In addition, Ps claimed that the minimum tax violates various constitutional rights, particularly religious freedom. The Tax Court ruled in favor of D. Ps appeal.

Issue. Does the AMT apply to taxpayers who do not have any tax preference items?

Held. Yes. Judgment affirmed.

♦ The statute in question clearly defined the calculation to determine alternative minimum tax and left no room for interpretation. If Congress had intended to tax only preferences, it would have defined "alternative minimum taxable income" differently.

♦ Furthermore, the AMT does not unconstitutionally inhibit free exercise of religion. The fact that a generally applicable but neutral law may have the effect of making the observance of some religious beliefs more expensive does not make the statute unconstitutional under the First Amendment. Further, the uniform application of the AMT provisions furthers a compelling governmental interest. Hence, there is no equal protection or due process violation.

Comment. Note that the AMT exception is not indexed for inflation. As the concurrence notes, unless the tax is modified by Congress, more and more taxpayers will be subject to AMT in the future.

---

h. Job-related business expenses--

Prosman v. Commissioner, T.C. Memo. 1999-87.

Facts. As a computer consultant employee, the taxpayer (P) bid on different projects using a formula that included a standard hourly rate and a per diem allowance for out-of-town work. P requested that his employer separate his per diem allowance from his base rate. The employer refused and included both amounts as taxable wages on P's 1995 Form W-2. P filed his return, reporting the amount shown on the W-2, and then took an itemized deduction for the job expenses. For 1995, P reported total regular tax in the amount of $4,924. The Commissioner (D) determined that the itemized deductions resulted in an additional AMT liability of $2,688. P contends that D's application of the AMT under IRC section 55 is inequitable and should not be applied to P.

Issue. Is P subject to the AMT under section 55?

Held. Yes.

◆ P may be correct in asserting that if his employer had designated amounts paid as reimbursed employee business expenses, rather that as wages, P would not have incurred additional taxes under section 55. However, P negotiated the best contract that he could and his compensation must be taxed based on the manner in which it was received. It is clear that job-related business expenses deducted as itemized deductions must be added back to income in determining AMT.

VII. THE SPLITTING OF INCOME

A. INTRODUCTION

Generally, an item of income is taxed to the person who earned it or owns the producing property. But, due to the progressive tax rates, many attempts have been made to divide income among family members or other entities, and in so doing reduce the earner's tax liability.

B. INCOME FROM SERVICES: DIVERSION BY PRIVATE ARRANGEMENT

1. **Introduction.** Before Congress allowed income splitting between spouses in 1948, taxpayers were very creative in devising their own methods of splitting incomes. Tax advantages can still be attained by splitting income with children and other relatives. These include the ability to use lower tax rates as well as the advantage of additional personal exemptions.

2. **Do-It-Yourself Community Property--**

Lucas v. Earl, 281 U.S. 111 (1930).

Facts. Earl (D) entered into a contract with his wife by which they agreed that any income either of them earned would be owned by them as joint tenants. D claims that, due to his contract, he can be taxed only on one-half of his income. The Commissioner (P) and the Board of Tax Appeals held that D should be taxed on the whole of his income. The court of appeals reversed and P appeals.

Issue. Does a contract allow an earner of income to prevent his salary from vesting for tax purposes?

Held. No. Judgment reversed.

♦   Section 61(a) taxes the net income of every individual "derived from salaries, wages, or compensation for personal services." The statute does not seek to tax only income beneficially received, but that which is actually earned. One cannot, by agreement, attribute fruits to a different tree from that on which they grew.

---

3. **Services Rendered for Charity.** Often a radio station or motion picture producer will engage the services of a celebrity or performer, who will allow

the proceeds of his services to go to charity. This was seen as an alternative to claiming the proceeds as income and deducting the donation as a charitable contribution, the deduction being limited by the percentage limitation. Rev. Rul. 53-71 states that "if the individual does not participate directly or indirectly in the contract pursuant to which his services are made available to the third party and if he has no right to receive, or direct the use or disposition of, the amounts so paid, such amounts are not includible in his gross income." The principles applied to charities have been extended to political organizations in Rev. Rul. 68-503, 1968-2 C.B. 44.

C. INCOME FROM SERVICES: DIVERSION BY OPERATION OF LAW

1. Community Property.

a. Introduction--

Poe v. Seaborn, 282 U.S. 101 (1930).

Facts. Seaborn's (P's) income came from salary, interest, dividends, and profits from real property sales. P and his wife lived in a community property state wherein the wife had a vested interest as co-owner of all earnings accruing to the husband after marriage. P and his wife each claimed one-half of the year's income on their respective returns. The Commissioner (D) determined that P should claim all of the income on his return, but the district court held for P. D appeals.

Issue. In a state where a taxpayer's income is community property, may each spouse claim one-half of the income on his or her tax return?

Held. Yes. Judgment affirmed.

♦ In a state in which the wife has a vested property right in the community property, and in the community income, equal to her husband, each spouse may file a separate tax return treating one-half of the community income as his or her own.

---

b. **The burden of community property.** A spouse may be taxed on one-half of the other spouse's earnings in a community property state even though she did not get any benefit from it. Also, in *United States v. Mitchell*, 403 U.S. 190 (1971), it was held that a wife could not escape liability for her half of the community income by a subsequent renunciation of her community rights.

c. **Common law states.** If a husband makes a gift to his wife, the subsequent income from the property is taxed to her. If the property is put into joint tenancy, the income is divided between the two. However, earned income cannot be split, and subsequent income from gifted property may be attributed to the grantor spouse if she retains exclusive control over it.

2. Income Splitting by Congressional Grace.

a. **Taxation of married couples and single persons.** From 1948 to 1969, married couples were allowed to split their income as if each spouse had earned one-half of the total. The 1948 law came in response to the inequities which existed since community property states (unlike common law states) allowed married couples to split their income regardless of who actually earned it. The 1948 Act gave married individuals an advantage over single taxpayers, no two of whom could split their incomes to lower their tax rates. In response to this, in 1969 Congress enacted a lower single taxpayer rate schedule. Thus, a single taxpayer is taxed at rates 17% to 20% above those for married *couples* with similar incomes. This compromise has both sides complaining. Single taxpayers bemoan the income splitting afforded married taxpayers, while the latter group bemoans the lower rates afforded singles. Beginning in 2005, the standard deduction and the 15% tax bracket will be gradually increased for married taxpayers to reduce the marriage penalty.

b. **Income of children.** A dependent child's income is taxable to him and not his parents (although the parents must see that the tax is paid). Under section 151(e), a child may be claimed as a dependent even though he earns over the exemption amount if he is under 19 or is a student. This, however, is true only if the taxpayer furnishes over one-half of the dependent's support costs.

c. **Heads of households and surviving spouses.** The income splitting allowed married persons in 1948 seemed particularly unfair to the single person with dependents, such as a widow with children. In 1969, a new reduced rate was granted to any single person supporting in her own household a child or any other person who qualifies as a dependent.

d. **Married persons filing separate returns.** Section 1(d) provides rates for married persons who file separate returns. Generally, it would be advantageous for married persons to file separate returns only in a situation where a limitation, such as the 7.5% floor on medical expenses, could be avoided in one of the returns because of the relationship of the two incomes.

D. INCOME FROM SERVICES: MORE ON DIVERSION BY PRIVATE ARRANGEMENT

1. Assignment for Third Parties--

Armantrout v. Commissioner, 67 T.C. 996 (1977), *aff'd per curiam*, 570 F.2d 210 (7th Cir. 1978).

Facts. Armantrout (P) was one of several key employees of Hamblin Inc., an electronics firm. Hamblin entered into an agreement whereby a fund was set up out of which the education expenses of key employees' children would be paid. A maximum of $10,000 would be paid to all of the children of a key employee, with limitations for each child. The program was used as a recruiting inducement by Hamblin to attract personnel for key positions. Compensation for key employees without children was not increased to equalize benefits available to other employees through the fund. The Commissioner (D) ruled that plan benefits were taxable compensation to P and others since the benefits were not geared to scholastic performance by the children but were treated as employment benefits.

Issue. Are the amounts received by children under an education fund of this type attributable to the parent-employees?

Held. Yes. Judgment for D.

♦ When a benefit is created in an employment situation and in connection with the performance of services, the benefit must be classified as income. Anticipatory arrangements designed to deflect income from the proper taxpayer will not be given effect to avoid tax liability.

♦ By accepting employment or continuing to be employed by Hamblin, with the fund payments in mind, P consented in effect to having his earnings paid to third parties. P was thus in a position to influence the manner in which his compensation was paid. Agreeing to the plan was an "anticipatory arrangement" prohibited by *Lucas v. Earl.*

E. TRANSFERS OF PROPERTY AND INCOME FROM PROPERTY

1. The *Blair* Rule--

Blair v. Commissioner, 300 U.S. 5 (1937).

Facts. Blair (P) was to receive the income from a trust created by his father. P assigned interests in the trust to his children. The trustees accepted the assignments and paid the trust income directly to the assignees. The Commissioner (D) held the assignments to be taxable to P, but the Board of Tax Appeals reversed his decision. The court of appeals then reversed, and P appeals its decision.

Issue. Can a beneficiary avoid taxation on trust income by assigning his interests in the trust to others?

Held. Yes. Judgment reversed.

♦　　　The one who is to receive the income as the owner of the beneficial interest is to pay the tax. If the interest is assignable without reservation, the assignee thus becomes the beneficiary. P's interest in the trust was present property alienable like any other. P could thus transfer a part of his interest as well as the whole. Here, the assignees became the owners of a specified beneficial interest, a form of property (not a chose in action), and the income arising therein is taxable to them.

2.　*Blair* Rule Application--

Helvering v. Horst, 311 U.S. 112 (1940).

Facts. Horst (D) owned bonds with detachable interest coupons. D delivered the coupons to his son as a gift. When the coupons matured, D's son cashed them. The Commissioner (P) and the Board of Tax Appeals held D taxable for the bond interest. The court of appeals reversed, and P appeals.

Issue. Should the donor be taxed for bond interest when he gave the interest coupon to another before maturity?

Held. Yes. Judgment reversed.

♦　　　Income is realized by the assignor when he diverts the payment which he could have received to the donee. This fulfills a want of the donor who, in a real sense, enjoys compensation from such fulfillment.

Dissent (McReynolds, J.). The interest coupons were independent items of property from the bonds. When the coupons were given to the son, they became his absolute property.

---

3. **Analysis.** It is possible to distinguish *Blair* and *Horst* by analyzing to what extent the donor in each case retained the corpus or the source of the income. In *Horst,* despite the dissenter's view that the coupons were independent of the bonds, the bonds were the actual source of the income. In *Blair*, the donor assigned an interest in a trust. The Court stated, "The assignment of the beneficial interest is not the assignment of a chose in action but of the 'right, title, and estate in and to property.'" A portion of the source of the income was given up by the donor in *Blair.* In *Horst,* this corpus was retained by the donor. Some have felt that the Supreme Court bent this rationale to its logical extreme in these two holdings.

F. SERVICES TRANSFORMED INTO PROPERTY

1. **The Gift of Compensation or Property Accruing from Personal Services--**

Helvering v. Eubank, 311 U.S. 122 (1940).

Facts. Eubank (P), an insurance agent, had a right to continue commissions when life insurance policies that he sold were renewed. In 1924 and 1928, P assigned his renewal commissions to others. The assignments were made after P terminated his employment and before the taxable year when he would have received the assigned income. The Commissioner (D) taxed the income to P, but a lower court held that the income was not taxable to P. D appeals.

Issue. Is a right to income assigned after the work is done but before the income is due taxable to the donor?

Held. Yes. Judgment reversed.

♦ If the assignment of income is made after the work is finished, the income is still taxable to the person who did the work.

---

2. **Earnings Refused in Favor of Another Recipient.** In *Commissioner v. Giannini,* 129 F.2d 638 (9th Cir. 1942), a corporate president refused part of his salary and suggested that the corporation do something worthwhile with the money. The court held that he was not taxable for the refused salary. Note that an unqualified refusal of the money was made with no specific request to pay the money to any particular donee. "So far as the taxpayer was concerned, the corporation could have kept the money."

3. **Gift of Property Which Is the Product of Services.** When a person writes a book or invents a product, he has produced property through his personal

efforts. However, the courts have not carried the *Eubank* holding to include such income from the property as personal service income. If the taxpayer gives the property to charity, he will not be taxed on its future royalties since "property" and not a "right to income" has been given away. This rationale may not hold if the asset produced is linked to personal services for another. For example, in *Strauss v. Commissioner,* 168 F.2d 441 (2d Cir. 1948), a taxpayer received a percentage of royalties in return for personal services in helping finance the "Kodachrome" process. He thereafter assigned the royalties. The circuit court held the royalty income arising after the assignment as taxable income to the taxpayer.

4. **Gift of Income and Property Rights--**

Heim v. Fitzpatrick, 262 F.2d 887 (2d Cir. 1959).

Facts. Heim (P) invented a new type of rod end and bearing which he patented. P transferred his rights to the patent to a company of which he was the principal owner. The company was to pay P royalties as the invention sold. He then assigned to his wife and children the majority of his royalty rights from the patent as well as other collateral rights. The Commissioner (D) decided that the royalties paid to P's family were actually income to P. In the Tax Court, P argued that the transfers were gifts of income-producing property and consequently the royalties arising from the property should be taxable to the donees. The Tax Court held for D, and P appeals.

Issue. Was a sufficient property right transferred to the donees so as to shift the income to them?

Held. Yes. Judgment reversed.

♦ In this case, P assigned to the donees more than a bare right to receive future royalties. The power to fix royalties on new types of bearings and a reversionary interest in the invention was also given to the donees. The rights assigned to the wife and children donees were sufficiently substantial to justify the view that they were given income-producing property.

Comment. The assignment of patents and copyrights raises difficult questions. If the transferee is given the entire interest in the patent or copyright, the income is taxable to him. Generally, however, a transfer of a bare license to receive royalties from a patent or copyright leaves the royalty income taxable to the donor.

---

5. **Analysis.** Note the increased sophistication in taxpayers' attempts to maintain control and benefit over property held in trust during this time in cases like *Helvering v. Clifford,* 309 U.S. 331 (1940). Also note the applications

of the *Blair* Rule in *Horst* and *Eubank.* The early judicial decisions established the following general principles:

a.   Income from services should be attributed to the earner.

b.   Income from property should be attributed to the owner of the property.

c.   Income from other sources should be attributed to the person to whom the income belongs (for example, an injured or subsidized taxpayer).

d.   In cases where the recipient of the income is not the income earner or property owner, the interests of each contributing party are weighed to determine whose interest is the most significant. The entire income is then taxed to that person.

G.   TRUSTS

1.   **Introduction.** Subchapter J of the Code addresses the taxation of income earned by trusts. Parts A through D govern situations where either the trust or the beneficiaries are taxable, while part E governs the rules that attribute income to the grantor. Some of the cases in the preceding chapter laid the judicial foundation for the grantor trust rules. These will be discussed in more detail below.

2.   **Trusts Where Income Is Not Taxable to the Grantor or Another Person as an Owner.** Assuming that the grantor has not retained substantial "strings" or powers over the trust, the trust itself will be recognized as a separate taxable entity. Generally, the income that is distributed to the beneficiaries is taxed to them. The trust pays tax only on the income it retains. The taxable income of a trust is known as distributable net income ("DNI"). This is the net income of the trust without deducting distributions to beneficiaries or undistributed capital gains allocated to the trust corpus. Except for these and a few other modifications, the DNI is the trust's net income.

   a.   **Simple trusts.**

      1)   **Definition.** A trust that requires all of its income to be distributed to the beneficiaries without adding any of the income to the trust corpus is a simple trust. Also, to qualify as a simple trust, no amount of income may be used for charitable purposes. [I.R.C. §651(a)]

      2)   **Taxation.** In a simple trust, income is taxed to the beneficiaries instead of to the trust. This is done by giving the trust a deduction for all distributions made during the year. The trust's DNI is the maximum amount that the trust may deduct or that the beneficiaries can be taxed on. For example, if trust income (under state law)

were $5,600 but DNI were only $5,000, the excess $600 could be distributed tax-free.

b.   Complex trusts.

1)   Definition. If the trustee has the discretionary power to distribute or accumulate income or to distribute trust corpus, the trust is a complex trust.

2)   Taxation. I.R.C. section 662(a) uses a two-tier approach in taxing complex trusts. Distributions are classified into the first or second tier.

   a)   First tier. Income that is required to be currently distributed is a first tier distribution.

   b)   Second tier. Discretionary amounts that the trustee allows to be paid to certain beneficiaries are second tier distributions.

   c)   Example. DNI is allocated to the first tier distributions, with the remainder prorated among the second tier. Suppose that DNI is $13,000 and the trust instrument requires $10,000 to be paid to A. The trustee decides to make discretionary payments of $4,000 to B and $2,000 to C. A's entire distribution is taxable under the first tier. This leaves only $3,000 available for the second tier which is prorated between B and C. B is taxed on $2,000 and C on $1,000.

c.   The unlimited throwback rule. A low tax bracket trust used to be a good tax savings device. A high bracket taxpayer would allow trust income to accumulate in the trust and the trust would be taxed on it at lower rates. Then, in subsequent years, the taxpayer could receive the income tax-free to the extent that it exceeded the subsequent year's DNI. The throwback rules [I.R.C. §§665 through 668] take away this tax-saving device. The rule states that when a trust distributes accumulated income, it will be taxed to the beneficiaries as if it had been received by them in the earliest tax year in which the trust had undistributed net income.

d.   Multiple trusts. I.R.C. section 643(e) provides that multiple trusts that incorporate the same grantor and beneficiary, and have as their principal motive tax avoidance, shall be consolidated and treated as one trust. This, along with the throwback rule, mitigates any tax advantage of multiple trusts.

e.   Charitable trusts.

1)   Charitable remainder trusts. A taxpayer could set up a trust whereby the trust income was to be paid to private beneficiaries with the remainder going to charity. Under previous law, the taxpayer could claim a charitable contribution for the present value of the charitable interest. This type of trust was subject to abuses since the remainder could be contingent or subject to the trustee's invasion power. Thus, the charitable organization often did not get the full contribution that the taxpayer deducted. Sections 642 and 664 of the Code do not allow charitable trusts with a noncharitable income beneficiary unless the trust is in the form of either an "annuity trust" or a "unitrust" (*see* 3), 4), below).

2) **Charitable income trusts with noncharitable remainder.** If a taxpayer sets up a trust with a charity as the income beneficiary with a noncharitable remainder, he could attain a double tax benefit. He could claim a charitable contribution for the income given to the charity without having to claim the trust income. Sections 642 and 664 allow this form of trust only if it follows the "annuity trust" or "unitrust" requirements.

3) **The annuity trust.** This type of trust requires that the income beneficiary each year receive a percentage of at least 5% of the fair market value of the trust assets. This protects the income beneficiary against loss in the value of the trust corpus.

4) **The unitrust.** In this trust, the income beneficiary's annual distribution is computed by valuing the trust assets each year, of which he receives a stated percentage. This form of trust is a good protection against inflation.

f. **The grantor trust rules.** It is well established that if a person makes an outright gift of property, the income tax consequences generally follow the property. However, many donors make gifts with strings attached. Where the grantor holds excessive controls over the property, the income of such property is taxed to the grantor. The principle of excessive grantor controls was vague and became administratively unwieldy. Consequently, Congress enacted sections 671 through 678, which now are the criteria for deciding whether trust income should be taxed to the grantor.

1) **Reversionary interests.** Before 1987, section 673 taxed the grantor for trust income if he retained a reversionary interest taking effect within 10 years. However, the Tax Reform Act of 1986 eliminated the 10-year reversion rule. The new law states that a grantor will be taxed on the income of the trust if he has a reversionary interest with a value greater than 5% of the value of the trust.

2) **Power to revoke or alter the trust.**

a)   **In general.** Section 676 states that if the grantor or other nonadverse party (*i.e.*, nonbeneficiary) has the power to revoke the trust within 10 years after its inception and revest all or part of the corpus in the grantor, he is taxable for the trust income. Section 674 states that if the parties above have control over *who* gets the corpus or income or *when* it will be available, the income is taxable to the grantor. However, independent trustees, although nonadverse, may apportion income or corpus among beneficiaries without coming under the section 674 restriction.

b)   **Controls over beneficial enjoyment not deemed excessive.** The following powers are deemed reasonable controls and will not cause trust income to be taxed to the grantor, even if retained by the grantor himself:

(1)   Section 674(b)(5) states that the trust corpus may be invaded for the benefit of a designated beneficiary if such power is limited by a reasonably definite standard.

(2)   Section 674(b)(3) allows the grantor to alter the disposition of income in his will.

(3)   Section 674(b)(6) allows the grantor to control the distribution or accumulation of income. However, the accumulated income must eventually be paid to the same beneficiary who would have received it currently.

(4)   Section 674(b)(7) allows the grantor to postpone payments to a minor or other beneficiary under a legal disability.

c)   **Tentative trusts.** In Rev. Rul. 62-148, 1962-2 C.B. 153, the IRS ruled that income on funds deposited in a savings account in the depositor's name as "trustee" for another person is taxable to the depositor if, under local law, a revocable trust is created.

3)   **Power to divert income for the grantor's benefit.** Section 677 makes the grantor taxable for trust income if he or a nonadverse party has the power to apply the income for the benefit of the grantor or grantor's spouse. This includes premiums on the grantor's life or to aid in supporting the grantor's dependents.

4)   **Other powers that may benefit grantor.** Section 675 taxes the grantor if he has powers over the trust exercisable for his own benefit. For example, if the grantor could borrow cash from the

trust interest-free, he would be considered the owner of the trust for tax purposes.

5) **Demand trusts.** A demand trust is created when someone other than the grantor is given the right to demand the income or corpus of a trust for her own benefit. If grandparents created a trust with their grandchildren as income beneficiaries, but gave their children the right to demand that the income be paid to them, their children would be treated as the owners of the demand trust. Consequently, I.R.C. section 678 would tax the children on the income of the trust.

H. UNIFORM GIFTS TO MINORS ACT

Rev. Rul. 59-357, 1959-2 C.B. 212, holds that income from property transferred under the Model Gifts of Securities to Minors Act (Model Gifts Act) that is used in satisfaction of or to discharge the legal obligation of any person shall be taxed to such person to the extent so used. The Model Gifts Act allows the custodian to use the income for the support, maintenance, and general use of the minor. The Uniform Gifts to Minors Act somewhat limits the powers of the custodian. However, the IRS holds that Rev. Rul. 59-357 also applies to the Uniform Gifts to Minors Act.

I. FAMILY PARTNERSHIPS

1. **Taxation of Partnership in General.** Sections 701 through 771 (subchapter K) of the Code cover partnerships. Partnerships are not subject to income tax, but are required to file tax returns showing net income or loss. The individual partners are subject to income tax on their shares of the partnership income. For this reason, the partnership is considered to be a "conduit" through which the partnership income or loss flows through to the individual partners. The individual partner, however, does not merely claim the single net figure of his tax return. The separate characterizations of income and loss retain their nature as they are taken by each partner. Thus, one partner could claim a long-term capital gain as well as an ordinary operating loss from the same partnership. The character of an item of income or deduction is determined at the partnership level, without regard to the individual partners who ultimately claim the item.

2. **Family Partnerships.** In *Commissioner v. Culbertson*, 337 U.S. 733 (1949), the Court addressed what was required for a family partnership to be recognized for tax purposes. The Court held that to become a bona fide member of a family partnership, it was not enough that a partner contributed either vital services or original capital. Most important was a showing by the partners that they acted in good faith and with a business purpose in entering into the

family partnership. A business purpose had to be something more than tax avoidance. Congress substantially relaxed the requirements of *Culbertson*. Where capital is a "material income-producing fact" in the partnership, the gift will effectively shift income, even if the donee contributes neither capital nor services.

J. GIFT AND LEASEBACK

1. Landmark Case--

Brooke v. United States, 468 F.2d 1155 (9th Cir. 1972).

Facts. Brooke (P) was a physician who, by 1959, had a family with six children. P gifted real estate to his children which included a pharmacy, rental apartment, and medical offices. After the conveyance, the Montana State Probate Court appointed P as guardian of the children. In this capacity, P collected rents from the pharmacy and apartment, and paid to himself as the children's guardian the reasonable rental value of his medical offices. The rents were applied to the children's health insurance, school tuition, musical instruments, swimming and speaking lessons, and an automobile for P's oldest child. The Commissioner (D) disallowed P's deduction of rental payments under section 162(a)(3) as ordinary and necessary business income expenses, arguing that an insufficient property interest had been transferred to the children.

Issue. In this gift and leaseback, was a sufficient property interest transferred from P to the donee-children?

Held. Yes. Judgment affirmed.

♦   In analyzing a gift and leaseback, the factors to be considered are as follows:

The duration of the transfer: In this case the transfer of property was by warranty deed, unconditioned and unencumbered. Thus, it was an absolute transfer of property.

Control is retained by the donor: Few, if any controls over the trust property were retained by P. He was obligated to pay a reasonable rent for his medical offices. Also, P could at any time be terminated as guardian.

Use of the property for the donor's benefit: In this case trust benefits have not inured to the taxpayer as donor. P was not legally obligated to provide these benefits for his children.

The trustee's independence: Since the Montana Probate Court administered the guardianship in this case, rental obligations were required to be met, and guardianship property could not be sold without court approval.

♦ In this case, P desired to provide for the health and education of his children, avoid friction with partners in his medical practice, withdraw his assets from the threat of malpractice, and diminish the ethical conflicts arising from owning a medical practice with a pharmacy. This is sufficient economic reality or business purpose to justify the gift and leaseback.

Dissent. The majority in this case has disregarded our own prior decisions with regard to gift and leaseback transactions. Tax consequences are determined not from the formal aspect of a transaction, but from the actual substance of a piece of business. What is found here lacks business meaning for tax purposes. [Kirschenmann v. Westover, 255 F.2d 69 (9th Cir.), *cert. denied,* 350 U.S. 834 (1955)] In this case there was no legitimate business purpose motivating the transfer of the lease property.

---

2. **Subsequent Holdings.** In *Rosenfeld v. Commissioner,* 706 F.2d 1277 (2d Cir. 1983), a taxpayer established a 10½-year trust for the benefit of his children. In the trust, he contributed a building that he occupied as a physician. In that case the trust was upheld. The court rejected the theory that there must be a business purpose for the gift and leaseback together, concluding that a business purpose for the leaseback alone was sufficient.

K. SHIFTING INCOME WITH THE USE OF CORPORATIONS

1. **Shifting Income Through a Corporation**

   a. **Introduction.** When a shareholder gives shares to a family member, but retains an active role in the management of the corporation, the donor's interest and control in the corporation remain unchanged. If such a transfer is a mere assignment of dividend income, it will be reallocated to the donor.

   b. **Corporate formalities--**

Foglesong v. Commissioner, 621 F.2d 865 (7th Cir. 1980).

Facts. Foglesong (P) was a highly successful salesman of steel tubing. In 1966, P formed a corporation of which he held 98 shares, and his wife and an accountant close friend held one share each. In the tax years in question, the corporation paid no dividends. It also issued preferred stock to P's four minor children, and issued preferred dividends of $32,000 during the four-year period. During the years in question, the net receipts of the corporation were as much as three times the salary that the corporation paid P. During this time, the corporation complied with all of the formalities required of such an entity, such as holding proper meetings, maintaining bank accounts, and employing a secretary. The Tax Court held that tax avoidance considerations far outweighed any genuine business concerns of the taxpayer in setting up the corporation. However, the Tax Court found the corporation to be a viable entity. Notwithstanding this finding, the court substantially disregarded the corporation for tax purposes.

Issue. Should business considerations be weighed against those of tax avoidance in determining whether a corporation should be disregarded?

Held. No. Judgment reversed and case remanded.

♦ In this case, the following circumstances are present to indicate the viability of the corporation: (i) the corporation was a party to service contracts; (ii) the corporation was not looked upon as a sham; (iii) nontax purposes were present as a major concern in forming the corporation; (iv) the corporation was not formed for the purpose of taking advantage of losses incurred by a separate trade or business; (v) the corporate form had been consistently followed; (vi) P rendered services exclusively for the corporation; (vii) the corporation was not disqualified from performing the services required of it under the contract; (viii) the parties paying for P's services were not controlled by P; and (ix) other appropriate legal bases, such as limitation of liability, were reasons for forming the corporation.

♦ An attempt to strike a balance between tax avoidance motives and "legitimate" business purposes is unproductive and inappropriate. Such an approach places too little value on the policy of the law to recognize corporations as accepted economic entities.

♦ In this case, section 482 of the Code or another assignment of income doctrine should be applied to reallocate income, deductions, credits, or allowances among taxpayers to prevent evasion of taxes.

Dissent. This is a make-believe corporation. I would affirm the holding of the Tax Court.

---

2. **Shifting Income to a Corporation.**

   a. **Objective.** A frequent income-shifting scheme is to form a corporation with the objective of shifting income from the shareholder-individual to the corporation. The advantages of such a shift include: (i) the lower corporate tax rates, and (ii) the advantage of qualified pension and profit-sharing plans readily available in a corporate setting not available to individuals. For this reason, self-employed doctors and lawyers often incorporate with the sole objective of shifting income.

b. **Loan-out corporations invalid.** In *Johnson v. Commissioner*, 78 T.C. 882 (1982), the taxpayer was a professional basketball player with the San Francisco Warriors. He contracted with a corporation as a tax planning vehicle. In the contract he agreed to perform services exclusively for his corporation. Johnson expected to have his corporation enter into a contract with the basketball club, with Johnson guaranteeing performance of the contract. This is commonly known as a "loan-out" corporation. In Johnson's case, the Warriors were unwilling to contract with his corporation; instead they demanded to have a contract with Johnson. Johnson complied and the Tax Court later held that the salary payments were taxable to him rather than to his corporation.

L. PENSION TRUSTS

1. In General--

United States v. Basye, 410 U.S. 441 (1973).

Facts. A group of over 200 physicians organized a partnership ("Permanente"). The partnership agreed to provide medical services to a health plan's (Kaiser's) members. As part payment, the plan contributed to the partnership's retirement plan at a predetermined rate. The fund was contained in a trust. No beneficiary doctor could receive funds prior to retirement; also, trust income did not vest until then. From 1959 to 1963, Kaiser paid over $2 million to the trust, but neither the partnership nor the partners reported any income. The Commissioner assessed deficiencies to each partner for his or her distributive share of partnership income. The partners, including Basye (P), filed for a refund and brought suit. The Commissioner appeals a judgment for P.

Issue. Are anticipatory assignments of personal services income valid for income tax attribution?

Held. No. Judgment reversed.

♦ Here the partnership earned the income and, through a previous agreement, it was diverted to a trust. A long-held rule of taxation is that the entity earning income cannot avoid taxation by entering into a contract whereby the income is diverted to some other entity.

Comment. Note the reaffirmation of *Lucas v. Earl* here and the strict limitation of *Commissioner v. First Security Bank of Utah*, 405 U.S. 394 (1972), that the holding in this case indicates.

VIII. CAPITAL GAINS AND LOSSES

A. BACKGROUND

Prior to 1986, capital gains were given preferential tax treatment. Taxpayers were allowed a deduction of 60% of net long-term capital gains. However, capital losses were unfavorably treated. Capital losses were limited to offsetting capital gains plus $3,000 of ordinary income. The Tax Reform Act of 1986 repealed the 60% deduction and placed the ceiling rate on ordinary income and capital gains at 28%. Subsequent tax acts raised the upper rate on ordinary income first to 31% and then to 39.6%, while retaining the 28% ceiling rate on capital gains.

Currently, the maximum long-term capital gains tax rate for individuals is 15%, while ordinary income is subject to a maximum tax rate of 35%. For individuals in the 15% ordinary income tax bracket, long-term capital gains are only taxed at 10%. As a consequence, taxpayers must still characterize gains and losses as capital or ordinary to determine the proper tax rates to apply and/or to determine the amount of losses allowed. In addition, the capital gain rules are still important in recovery-of-basis situations.

B. THE STATUTORY FRAMEWORK

1. **The Mechanics.** (Refer to accompanying illustration below.) In order to have gains and losses, first the taxpayer must determine whether he has "realized" gain or loss from the "sale or exchange" of a "***capital asset.***" The precise meaning of these terms is discussed below. Then it must be determined whether the gain or loss realized must be "recognized." The gain or loss is then computed by subtracting the adjusted basis from the amount realized. The adjusted basis is the property's basis (acquisition cost) ***plus*** other capitalized expenditures (*i.e.*, amounts not deductible as current expenses) ***less*** depreciation and other receipts chargeable to the capital account. The amount realized from the sale of a capital asset is the sum of money received on sale plus the fair market value of any property received.

    a. **Noncorporate taxpayers.** To arrive at the net gain or loss on capital transactions, the individual taxpayer follows these steps:

        1) **Segregate long-term and short-term transactions.** Capital assets that a taxpayer sells or exchanges before he has held them for more than one year are treated differently than "long-term" capital assets (*i.e.*, those capital items held for more than one year). *Note*: For assets acquired between June 22, 1984 and January 1, 1988, the holding period for long-term gain or loss is six months.

        2) **Net the amounts.** After the transactions are segregated by term, the short-term capital gains and losses are netted to reach a net

short-term capital gain (or loss). The same is done with the long-term transactions to arrive at a net long-term capital gain or loss. The tax treatment depends on the amounts and classifications of the net long-term and net short-term amounts.

a) **Net short-term capital gain exceeds net long-term capital loss.** Where this occurs, the excess short-term amount is treated as ordinary income.

b) **Net long-term capital gain exceeds net short-term capital loss.** The excess long-term capital gain is included in gross income. For example, suppose a taxpayer has taxable income of $15,000 and capital gains and losses as follows:

Long-term capital gain	-	$5,000
Long-term capital loss	-	$1,000
Short-term capital gain	-	$2,000
Short-term capital loss	-	$3,500

Netting the amounts would give the taxpayer a net long-term capital gain of $4,000 and a net short-term capital loss of $1,500. The excess of net long-term capital gain is therefore $2,500. This total is added to ordinary income to arrive at a gross income of $17,500.

c) **Both short-term and long-term gains.** If both net amounts show gains, the combined amount is included in gross income.

d) **Net short-term capital loss exceeds net long-term capital gain.** I.R.C. section 1211 allows up to $3,000 of the excess net capital loss to be deducted against ordinary income. The excess must be carried over to future years.

e) **Net long-term capital loss exceeds net short-term capital gain.** The same rules as in d), above, apply.

f) **Both short-term and long-term losses.** If both netted amounts show losses, the short-term loss is used first against the $3,000 ceiling. Excess amounts are carried over to future years.

b. **Corporate taxpayers.** Corporations determine their net capital gains and losses the same way as noncorporate taxpayers.

1) **Net capital gains.** Under prior law, the excess of net long-term capital gains over net short-term capital losses was subject to an alternative tax of 28%. This aided only those corporations whose

tax rate on ordinary income exceeded 28%. Beginning in 1987, corporations get no preferential treatment on capital gains.

2) **Net capital losses.** I.R.C. section 1211(a) allows corporations to deduct capital losses only to offset capital gains. The amount that is not used to offset capital gains may be carried back three years and forward five years and offset against those years' capital gains.

How Losses Are Utilized

	Individual	Corporation
Net operating loss	carry back 3 years and forward 15 years *or* elect to carry forward 15 years only	same as individual
Capital loss	carry forward forever	carry back 3 years and forward 5 years

c. **I.R.C. section 1231.** This section is a means of allowing capital gain treatment for noninventory business investment assets. Remember that the capital gain provisions were designated to apply to gains and losses on the disposition of long-term investment property rather than dispositions resulting from the day-to-day operation of a business. I.R.C. section 1231 was enacted for the taxpayer who uses long-term "investment" property in his business. To qualify for I.R.C. section 1231, then, property must be more akin to long-term investment property than to short-term use as inventory or business property. In addition to this "investment" test, property must also not fall under other exclusions to qualify under section 1231. Depreciable personal property will not qualify if it is held "primarily for sale to customers in the ordinary course of business." The same exclusion applies to real property. If such property is inventory to the taxpayer or held for sale, it will not qualify under section 1231. It is extremely difficult to effectively assure whether a particular asset will qualify under section 1231's nebulous qualifications. The result of this is that the determination of what is a section 1231 asset has been left largely to judicial interpretation.

d. **Depreciation recapture.** Much of the property eligible for I.R.C. section 1231 treatment is also property which can be depreciated under

I.R.C. section 167 (discussed *supra*). Thus, a taxpayer could take ordinary depreciation deductions and then claim a capital gain upon disposition of the property. I.R.C. sections 1245 and 1250 were enacted to eliminate this taxpayer practice, which had the effect of converting ordinary income into capital gain. These sections require a taxpayer to report certain portions of section 1231 gain as ordinary income.

1) **I.R.C. section 1245.** This section requires that upon the sale of depreciable personal property, any gain realized is ordinary income to the extent of all depreciation deductions taken after 1963. For example, suppose a taxpayer bought a machine in 1970 for $20,000 and deducted $12,000 depreciation from 1970 to 1979. If, in 1979, he sells the machine for $23,000, the gain realized is $15,000. I.R.C. section 1245 requires that $12,000 of this gain be recognized as ordinary income. The remaining $3,000 receives capital gain treatment.

2) **I.R.C. section 1250.** This section requires that "additional" depreciation claimed on buildings be recaptured. This means any depreciation in excess of the straight-line rate. For example, suppose that a taxpayer purchased a commercial building in 1970 for $100,000. The building has an expected useful life of 50 years. When the building was sold in 1980, depreciation of $32,000 had been claimed. Of this, the straight-line amount was $20,000. If the building was sold for $85,000, the gain realized would be $17,000 since the basis at that date was $68,000. I.R.C. section 1250 requires that $12,000 of the $17,000 gain be recognized as ordinary income, since that amount represents accelerated depreciation over the straight-line rate. I.R.C. section 1250(a)(1)(B) relaxes the recapture rule for low-income renters. If such buildings are held for over 100 months, the amount of recapture is decreased by 1% for each month held over 100 months. Therefore, if a low income housing unit were held for 120 months before being sold, 20% of the normally recaptured accelerated depreciation would be forgiven and the gain recognized to that extent would be capital gain.

C. THE POLICY OF CAPITAL GAINS

Increases in the value of capital assets are as much a part of income in terms of accretion as wages, salaries, rents, interest, royalties, and other gains or receipts. The question is often asked whether capital gains warrant, therefore, special or privileged treatment relative to other elements of income. Congress obviously had some important purpose in creating such a complex and constantly changing body of law. Listed below are some of the reasons that capital gains have been given favorable treatment in the past by Congress.

1. **Bunching of Income.** Gains realized in one year that have accrued (been earned) over a period of years subject the taxpayer to unfairly high tax rates under the graduated income tax structure.

2. **Inflation.** In a period of inflation, capital gains are at least partly not real income to the extent that they merely reflect the rise in general prices.

3. **Lock-in Effect.** Subjecting capital gains to a full tax induces investors to refrain from selling appreciated assets. This "lock-in" effect reduces liquidity and impairs the mobility of capital.

4. **Investment Deterrent.** Taxation of capital gains tends to deter investors' willingness to bear the risks of investment. Without a tax benefit to the investor, society must pay for risk-taking through the high price that would have to be paid for high-risk activities. This tends to slow the mobility of capital.

5. **Interest Rates.** When interest rates fluctuate, a portion of capital gain reflects a change in the rates at which income is capitalized, rather than reflecting true income.

D. DEFINITIONAL BACKDROP

1. **Introduction.** Recall that in order to fall under these rules, the asset must be a *"capital asset"* given up on a *"sale or exchange."* As you will see, the statutory law provides little guidance in resolving what qualifies under either definition. The Code should be kept in mind while reviewing the common law of capital gains and losses.

2. **Definitional Problems—Capital Assets.**

   a. **Introduction.** Capital gains or losses are derived only from the sale or exchange of property constituting a "capital asset." I.R.C. section 1221 includes all of a taxpayer's property as capital assets, with certain exceptions. The statutory exceptions include: (i) stock in trade or inventory of a business, (ii) depreciable property and real property used in a trade or business, (iii) literary or artistic property held by its creator, (iv) trade accounts or notes receivable, and (v) certain governmental obligations. The courts have construed the exceptions broadly in denying favorable capital gains treatment. However, taxpayers have used these cases as precedent in avoiding unfavorable capital loss treatment. The case law will be considered after studying the I.R.C. section 1221 exceptions.

   b. **The problem of distinguishing between investment and business.** I.R.C. section 1221(1) excludes from capital assets "stock in trade of the taxpayer or other property of a kind which would properly be included in the inventory of the taxpayer if on hand at the close of the taxable year, or property held by the taxpayer primarily for sale to customers in the ordinary course of his trade or business." This section attempts to exclude from capital gain treatment everyday profits of the business or commercial world. The distinction here is between profits of a "business" (which do not receive capital gain or loss treatment) and "investment" (which do). A sale of securities by an average investor would be looked upon as an investment, while the sale of inventory by a merchant would be a business sale. This is so despite the fact that inventory is "property" or "assets." This question has great areas of uncertainty beyond these obvious examples. A sale of an investment asset can have many of the trappings of a business sale.

E. PROPERTY HELD "PRIMARILY FOR SALE TO CUSTOMERS"

1. **Introduction.** Section 1221(1) *excludes* from capital asset treatment property "held by the taxpayer primarily for sale to customers in the ordinary course of his trade or business." Any gain or loss on the sale of such property is ordinary income.

   a. **No deal for trader--**

Bielfeldt v. Commissioner, 231 F.3d 1035 (7th Cir. 2000).

Facts. Bielfeldt (P) (whose wife is a party only because of a joint return), a United States Treasury notes and bonds trader, experienced approximately $85 million in losses in the 1980s and offset those losses against all but $3,000 a year in ordinary income. P claims to be a dealer rather than a trader; P claims his losses were connected with his dealer's "stock in trade," are treated as ordinary rather than capital losses, and can be fully offset against ordinary income. Capital losses can be fully offset against capital gains, but can be offset against ordinary income only up to $3,000 a year. The Commissioner (D) disallowed the offset; the Tax Court affirmed. P appeals.

Issue. Is P a dealer?

Held. No. Judgment affirmed.

♦ A dealer derives his income from the service he provides in the chain of distribution of the goods he buys and resells, not from the fluctuations in the market value of those goods. A trader's income is based on fluctuations in the market value of the securities or other assets that he trades. His income is dependent on the changes in the market value of his securities between the time he purchased them and the time he sells them.

♦ A dealer in securities is a stockbroker who owns shares that he sells to his customers at market price plus a commission. A floor specialist on one of the stock exchanges maintains an inventory in a particular stock to maintain liquidity. If its price rises, indicating that demand is greater than supply, he sells from his inventory to meet the additional demand, and if the price of the stock falls, he buys in the open market to provide a market for sellers. The stock market does not pay the specialist for this service; his income is derived from his purchase and sales and commissions on limit orders. The IRS code classifies him as a dealer. [*See* 26 U.S.C. §§1236 (a), (d)]

♦ P's securities are not sold on an organized exchange; there are no floor specialists. The market for Treasury securities is an over-the-counter market, like the NASDAQ. However, specialists on the organized exchanges perform a function that is independent of the form of the market, and dealers who specialize in Treasury securities ("primary dealers") are analogous to the floor specialists, like NASD market makers are. The Government Securities Act of 1986 even requires the primary dealers in Treasury securities, with some exceptions, to register with the SEC or the NASD. Although P is not a registered or primary dealer, P claims to perform the function of the specialist.

♦ P bought huge amounts of bonds and notes, hoarded them during the temporary glut on the market at the time of issue, and resold at a profit when the glut disappeared. He would often buy from and sell to the same dealers. P did not maintain an orderly market, did not maintain an inventory, skipped auctions that he speculated would not produce a glut, and for long periods of time had no inventory to sell because he participated in 6% to 15% of the auctions each year. Some years P was out of the market for as many as 200 days a year. His profit was purely the result of speculation.

---

2. "Primarily for Sale"--

Biedenharn Realty Co. v. United States, 526 F.2d 409 (5th Cir.), *cert. denied,* 429 U.S. 819 (1976).

Facts. Biedenharn (P) bought a plantation in 1935 for farming and investment. It was farmed until 1939, when several subdivisions were carved out of the land. The Commissioner (D) challenged P's contention that the land was held for investment and charged that it was held for resale. The district court held for P, stating that the land was originally held for investment. D appeals.

Issue. Can land which is held solely for subdividing and resale be called a capital asset?

Held. No. Judgment reversed. The following factors indicate that P was in the business of selling real estate:

♦ P's sales were frequent and substantial.

♦ P vigorously improved the property, adding streets, drainage, sewers, and utilities.

♦ Although P first intended the land to be held for investment, the change of purpose to subdivision and resale was entirely voluntary and not born of economic necessity.

Comment. Other factors viewed by the courts in distinguishing investment from resale are (i) solicitation and advertising efforts, and (ii) brokers' activities.

F. TRANSACTIONS RELATED TO THE TAXPAYER'S REGULAR BUSINESS

1. **Introduction.** Until recently, the *Corn Products* case, below, seemed to require an otherwise qualifying capital asset to be treated as ordinary if it was purchased as "an integral part of the taxpayer's business."

2. **The *Corn Products* Doctrine--**

Corn Products Refining Co. v. Commissioner, 350 U.S. 46 (1955).

Facts. Corn Products (P) manufactured products made from grain corn. At times, drought conditions forced P to purchase corn at an unprofitably high price. To avoid this, P began to purchase corn futures. P would take a contract on the futures as they were needed and sell the remainder if no shortage was imminent. P claimed that gains on these sales were capital gains made on investments. The Commissioner (D) found that the purchase of corn futures was an integral part of P's business and therefore gave rise to ordinary income. The Tax Court and court of appeals found P's futures transactions to be a hedge against shortages and an integral part of P's business. P appeals.

Issue. When a taxpayer's investments are an integral part of his business, should gain arising therefrom be given capital gain treatment?

Held. No. Judgment affirmed.

♦ P's futures investments were not those of a "legitimate capitalist" but of a farsighted manufacturer, made to insure against raw corn price increases. The purchase of futures was not made for speculative purposes, but to fill a raw materials manufacturing need.

♦ Congress intended that profits and losses arising from the everyday operation of a business be considered as ordinary rather than capital. The capital asset provisions should not be applied to defeat rather than further Congress's purposes.

---

3. Motive Irrelevant--

Arkansas Best Corp. v. Commissioner, 485 U.S. 212 (1988).

Facts. Arkansas Best Corp. (P) acquired 65% of the shares in the National Bank of Commerce between 1968 and 1974. Until 1972, the bank grew steadily and was a good investment. In 1972, the federal government declared the bank a problem because many of its outstanding loans were real estate loans and the market was declining. P continued to buy stock until 1975 when P sold the bulk of its stock in the bank. P claimed an ordinary loss deduction of $9,995,688 based upon the sale. The Commissioner (D) characterized the loss as a capital loss which subjected the loss to capital loss limitations. The Tax Court held that the stock purchased before 1972 was bought for investment purposes, making it a capital asset subject to a capital loss when sold. However, the stock bought subsequent to 1972 was purchased for the purpose of preserving the bank's business reputation. Since this was a business purpose, the stock was an ordinary asset subjected to an ordinary loss. The court of appeals affirmed in part and reversed in part, as it characterized all the stock as a capital asset subject to capital loss treatment.

Issue. Was the capital stock that P held a capital asset regardless of the purpose for which the stock was purchased?

Held. Yes. Judgment affirmed.

♦ P tried to argue that the *Corn Products* case created a general exemption from capital asset status for assets acquired for business purposes. However, *Corn Products* only stands for the concept that hedging transactions that are an integral part of a business-inventory purchase system fall within the inventory exclusion to items classified as capital assets. Since this case does not concern hedging, *Corn Products* does not apply.

♦ A taxpayer's motive for purchasing an asset is irrelevant to the question whether the asset is properly held and is thus within I.R.C. section 1221's general definition of a capital asset.

G. SUBSTITUTES FOR ORDINARY INCOME

1. **Introduction.** Income is chargeable to the person whose property or services earned the income. Thus, if a taxpayer sells the right to future income earned from his property, the proceeds (as a substitute for ordinary income) are not allowed capital gain treatment.

2. **Payment for Cancellation of a Lease--**

Hort v. Commissioner, 313 U.S. 28 (1941).

Facts. Hort (P) inherited a building subject to a long-term lease. One of P's tenants wished to terminate the lease prior to its expiration date. P settled the lease for $140,000 and claimed a deduction for the difference between the rental value of the unexpired lease term and the $140,000 actually received. The Commissioner (D) disallowed this "loss" and included the entire amount of the $140,000 in gross income. P filed suit for a refund. The Tax Court and the circuit court both affirmed the Commissioner's ruling. P appeals.

Issue. When a lessor receives cash compensation prior to the expiration of the lease term, and the amount received is less than the full rental payments that would have been received on the lease had it not been terminated, is the full amount received immediately recognizable as income?

Held. Yes. Judgment affirmed.

♦　　P received an amount of money in lieu of the future rental income he was entitled to under the lease.

♦　　The fact that P received less than he would have under the lease does not entitle him to a deduction for the difference.

♦　　The consideration received was not a return of capital. While a lease is a capital asset, the payments were a substitute for rental payments, not for the sale or exchange of the lease. Therefore, the gain recognized is ordinary income, not a return of capital.

Comment. The Supreme Court characterized the lessee's payment for cancellation of the lease as "nothing more than the relinquishment of the right to future rental payments."

---

3. **Lottery Rights--**

Womack v. Commissioner, 510 F.3d 1295 (11th Cir. 2007).

Facts. Womack (P) won a portion of an $8 million Florida State Lottery in 1996. The prize was payable in 20 annual installments of $150,000. P received the first four installments and reported them as ordinary income. In 2000, P sold the right to receive the remaining 16 payments for a lump sum payment of $1,328,000. P reported the lump sum payment as proceeds from the sale of a long-term capital asset. The Commissioner (D) claimed that the proceeds from the sale of rights to future installment payments from lottery winnings ("lottery rights") are not capital assets. P appeals.

Issue. Are lottery rights capital assets?

Held. No. Judgment affirmed.

♦ The Tax Court and the four federal circuit courts that have considered whether lottery rights are capital assets have concluded that they are not. These decisions are based on the substitute for ordinary income doctrine, which provides that when a party receives a lump sum payment as "essentially a substitute for what would otherwise be received at a future time as ordinary income," that lump sum payment is taxable as ordinary income.

♦ Congress intended ordinary income to be the default tax rate, and the term "capital asset" is to be construed narrowly in accordance with the purpose of Congress to afford capital-gains treatment only in situations typically involving the realization of appreciation in value accrued over a substantial period of time. This interpretation prevents taxpayers from circumventing ordinary income tax rates by selling rights to future ordinary income payments in exchange for a lump sum.

♦ The sale of a capital asset captures the increased value of the underlying asset. Lottery rights involve no underlying investment of capital, and any "gain" from their sale reflects no change in the value of the asset. It is simply the amount a taxpayer would have received eventually discounted to present value. A lottery winner who sells lottery rights transfers a right to income that is already earned, not a right to earn income in the future. On the other hand, a capital asset has the potential to earn income in the future, based on the owner's actions in using it.

♦ Proceeds from the sale of lottery rights are a clear substitute for ordinary income and are taxed as ordinary income.

4.   **Sale of Interest in a Trust--**

McAllister v. Commissioner, 157 F.2d 235 (2d Cir. 1946), *cert. denied,* 330 U.S. 826 (1947).

Facts. McAllister (P) owned a life estate in the income of a trust. She sold the life interest to the remainderman for $55,000, which was $8,790 less than the actuarial value of the life estate. P claimed a capital loss of that amount, asserting that the life estate was a capital asset that was transferred. The Commissioner (D) held that P merely received an advance payment of $55,000 taxable ordinary income. The Tax Court held for D, and P appeals.

Issue. Is a life estate a capital asset which receives capital gain or loss treatment at disposition?

Held. Yes. Judgment reversed and remanded.

♦　　　Had P held a fee interest, the assignment would have been regarded as the transfer of a capital asset. A life interest should not be treated differently.

♦　　　This case is distinguishable from *Hort v. Commissioner (supra)*, where a land-lord canceled a lease of nine years for a lump sum payment. A life estate is quite different from a mere right to anticipated rental income. The former is a durable property interest while the latter is only a right to future income.

Dissent. It is unlikely that Congress intended by the capital gain provisions to relieve a taxpayer of ordinary tax burdens as an incentive to destroy a trust.

5.　　Oil Payments--

Commissioner v. P.G. Lake, Inc., 356 U.S. 260 (1958).

Facts. Lake (P) is a corporation that produced oil and gas. In 1950, P owed its president $600,000. As cancellation of the debt, P assigned to its president an oil payment right of $600,000 plus interest at 3% per year, which was expected to become realized within three to four years. P reported the debt forgiveness as a capital gain in 1950. The Commissioner (D) assessed P with a tax deficiency, stating that the forgiven debt was ordinary income, subject to depletion. This case was consolidated with four others by the Court.

Issue. Is the right to receive income from mineral payments a capital asset?

Held. No. Judgment reversed.

- Here, there was no conversion of a capital asset. The lump sum received by P was essentially a substitute for what would otherwise be received in the future as ordinary income. The consideration was paid for the right to receive future income, not for an increase in the value of the income-producing property.

Comment. Section 636 now treats assignments such as the one in *Lake* as loans. Had this been in effect during *Lake,* P would not have recognized income until the oil payments were actually paid.

---

6.   **Bootstrap Sale to Charity--**

Commissioner v. Brown, 380 U.S. 563 (1965).

Facts. Brown (P) and his family sold a sawmill and lumber business to the California Institute of Cancer Research for $1,300,000, payable at $5,000 down, with the balance to be paid from the sawmill's profits over the succeeding 10 years, through notes to which the Institute had no personal liability for nonpayment. The Institute formed a new corporation (Fortuna) and leased the assets to it for five years. Fortuna was to pay 80% of its profits to the Institute, which would use 90% of this to pay off P. Four years later, Fortuna closed down. The Institute sold the lumber business and forwarded 90% of the proceeds to P. P received $936,131 of the amount owing to him, which the Commissioner (D) labeled as ordinary income. The Tax Court held the sale to be of a capital asset, and the appellate court affirmed.

Issue. If a purchaser is not personally liable for a debt covering an investment for which he paid nothing, is it a legitimate sale?

Held. Yes. Judgment affirmed.

- The fact that the Institute paid nothing for the business and assumed no risk for repayment is immaterial. Also, its lack of business control does not indicate a sham. The price paid for the business was fair and resulted from arm's length bargaining.

Concurrence (Harlan, J.). The seller gave something up and received something substantially different back. If words are to have meaning, there was a "sale or exchange."

Dissent (Goldberg, J., Warren, C.J., Black, J.). Giving credence to this transaction has allowed P to receive ordinary income of the corporation at capital gains rates. Since no risk shifting occurred, and since the payments were made from ordinary income, the transaction should not be given capital gains treatment.

Comment. The IRS now limits its attack on bootstrap sellers to cases where the purchase price is "excessive." [*See* Rev. Rul. 66-153, 1966-1 C.B. 187]

---

7.   **Franchises.** When a franchise is sold, an issue arises whether the franchise qualifies as a capital asset and whether the agreement qualifies as a sale or exchange. Section 1253 provides that the transfer of a franchise, trademark, or tradename is not to be treated as a sale or exchange of a capital asset if the transferor retains any significant power, right, or continuing interest with respect to the subject matter of the franchise, trademark, or tradename. In the usual franchise, the franchisor retains strict controls over the franchisee's operation. Payments received by the franchisor in such a situation are ordinary income.

8.   **Bootstrap Sales.** Before 1970, many taxpayers were able to convert ordinary income into capital gains through a "bootstrap" sale. To do so, first the stock of an incorporated business would be sold to a charity, which would pay the purchase price from the profits of the business. The charitable organization would then liquidate the corporation and lease the corporate assets to the seller, who formed a new corporation. The new corporation would pay a large part of its profits as rents to the charity, which would then pay it back to the original owners as installments on the original purchase. In 1969, Congress amended section 514 so that charitable organizations were taxed on income from debt-financed property. This took away most of the charitable organization's incentive to enter into such transactions.

9.   **Non-Interest Bearing Bonds or Notes.** When a non-interest bearing bond is issued at a discount, it is unknown what portion of the discount represents interest income (which is ordinary) and which portion represents future appreciation (which should be capital gain). I.R.C. section 1272 requires taxpayers who hold corporate bonds to prorate the original issue discount over the life of the bond and include a portion as ordinary income each year. As the discount is included in income each year, the basis in the bond is correspondingly increased. If the bondholder sells the bond prior to maturity, any gain over basis receives capital treatment. Note that this forces a cash basis taxpayer to use the accrual basis in amortizing the bond discount.

H. OTHER CLAIMS AND CONTRACT RIGHTS

1.   **Termination Payment--**

Baker v. Commissioner, 118 T.C. 452 (2002).

Facts. Baker (P) (husband) sold insurance only for State Farm Insurance. One of many "agent agreements" P signed provided that all property furnished to P by State Farm remained the property of State Farm, including information about policyholders. P's earnings were based on a percentage of net premiums. The agreement also provided that P or State Farm could terminate the agreement by written notice, that it would be terminated in the case of P's death, and that all of State Farm's property would be returned within 10 days of termination. P was entitled to termination payment based on the percentage of policies that either (i) remained in force after termination or (ii) were in force for the 12 months prior to termination. The agreement included a one-year covenant not to compete. P and State Farm did not negotiate the terms of the agreement. After approximately 34 years as an independent agent, P retired. He returned account information, computers, and other property to State Farm and the successor agent. In 1997, P received a payment of $38,622 from State Farm pursuant to the termination agreement and reported the payment as long-term capital gain on his 1997 return. P described the termination payment as an annuity payable over five years. The annuity was described as a sale of assets to State Farm that included "personally produced policies and other intangible assets." The Commissioner (D) determined the payment was ordinary income and disallowed it. D did not impose self-employment tax on the income. P brings this action.

Issue. Is the termination payment received by P upon retirement as an insurance agent of State Farm taxable as capital gain?

Held. No.

♦ Section 1222(3) defines a long-term capital gain as gain from the sale or exchange of a capital asset held for more than one year. "A 'capital asset' means property held by the taxpayer (whether or not connected with his trade or business) that is not covered by one of five specifically enumerated exclusions."

♦ D claims P did not sell any property because State Farm already owned the property; the property merely reverted to State Farm upon termination. We note that D did not determine that petitioners were liable for self-employment tax with respect to the termination payment.

♦ P argues that the payment was for the sale or buyout of a business. P claims that he established and protected a customer base for State Farm, developed goodwill and a going business concern, and that State Farm's termination payment is a buyout of P's business.

♦ We and the appeals court have previously held in similar cases that there are no "vendible business assets" in an insurance arrangement such as P's and the record did not support a finding of a sale of assets of a business. The court of appeals in *Schelble v. Commissioner,* 130 F.3d at 1388, observed that "even if the taxpayer had built up an organization of value, it was not his to sell since ... [the insurance company] under the contract owned all the property comprising such organization. As to the customer contacts. . . . [t]hey were not his to sell."

- For federal income tax purposes, whether there has been a sale is determined by whether the benefits and burdens of ownership have passed. Some of the factors considered are: (i) whether legal title passes; (ii) how the parties treat the transaction; (iii) whether an equity was acquired in the property; (iv) whether the contract creates a present obligation on the seller to execute and deliver a deed and a present obligation on the purchaser to make payments; (v) whether the right of possession is vested in the purchaser; (vi) which party pays the property taxes; (vii) which party bears the risk of loss or damage to the property; and (viii) which party receives the profits from the operation and sale of the property.

- Here, upon termination, P returned all property to State Farm pursuant to the agreement. P did not own the assets and could not have sold them. P's successor's assuming P's telephone number and hiring two of P's employees does not support P's argument. Nothing in the record indicated that P was paid for the successor's use of the telephone number or for the hiring of the employees.

- P owned no capital asset that he could sell to State Farm; thus, the termination payment does not represent gain from the sale or exchange of a capital asset.

- An amount received for an agreement not to compete is generally taxable as ordinary income. P entered into a covenant not to compete with State Farm and a portion of the termination payment was paid for the covenant not to compete.

---

2. **Sale of Contract Rights--**

Commissioner v. Ferrer, 304 F.2d 125 (2d Cir. 1962).

Facts. Ferrer (D) entered into a contract with the author of the novel *Moulin Rouge*, whereby D obtained various rights. Among these were (i) the exclusive right to present the play on stage, (ii) the right to prevent any disposition of the motion picture rights until November 1, 1951, and (iii) the right to receive 40% of the motion picture proceeds. Later, D sold his contractual rights to a production company and characterized the whole amount received as a capital gain. The Commissioner (P), claiming that the amount realized was ordinary income, brought suit in Tax Court, which held for D. P appeals.

Issue. Did the contractual rights which D sold give rise to capital gains?

Held. Yes as to (i) and (ii). No as to (iii). Judgment reversed and case remanded.

- There is no general rule to follow in identifying capital assets. However, one common characteristic of capital assets is that the owner has an estate encumbrance, or option to acquire an interest, in property which if itself held would be a capital asset. The ownership must be of something more than a right to obtain some contractual benefit.

♦ In this case, D had three rights by way of the contract. D's "lease" of the play created an enforceable right to enjoin others from interfering with this right. Likewise, D's power to prevent any motion picture production would be enforced in equity. These rights, therefore, are capital assets to D.

♦ However, D's right to receive 40% of the motion picture proceeds did not give him any legal or equitable right over the motion picture other than the right to the proceeds. Therefore, this third right does not constitute a capital asset. The case is remanded to determine the percentage of gain applicable to each contract right.

Comment. In prior cases, the Second Circuit has relied on the "sale or exchange" requirement in holding that cancellation of a contract right produced ordinary income. In *Ferrer*, the court ignores the method of transfer in favor of an analysis of the nature of the rights transferred.

---

3. **Privacy and Exploitation--**

Miller v. Commissioner, 299 F.2d 706 (2d Cir.), *cert. denied*, 370 U.S. 923 (1962).

Facts. Miller (P) granted Universal Pictures the right to film *The Glenn Miller Story* based on the life of her husband. P received royalty payments from the film's receipts, which she claimed represented capital gains. The Commissioner (D) held that the rights which she held on the story of her husband's life were not section 1221 property.

Issue. Is a spouse's public image a capital asset?

Held. No. Judgment affirmed.

♦ Universal could have produced the film without P's consent. The fact that it paid her to do so does not make her interest a property right. What Universal paid for was not property.

Comment. In 1977, district courts in New York and Tennessee recognized a property right in the name and likeness of a deceased entertainer.

---

4. **Patents, Copyrights, and the Like.** Section 1231(3) excludes from the definition of capital assets copyrights, literary or artistic compositions, and letters of memoranda in the hands of the creator. Such properties are not capital assets in the hands of the taxpayer whose personal effort created them. However, an inventor, purchaser, or legatee who acquires such property is allowed to treat it as capital property unless he purchased the property primarily for resale in the ordinary course of business. Section 1235 provides that a patent is a capital asset in the hands of the inventor or financier of the invention. Hence, patents are given preferred treatment over copyrights or other literary or artistic property.

I. BAILOUT OF CORPORATE EARNINGS

1. **Introduction--**

Gregory v. Helvering, 293 U.S. 465 (1935).

Facts. Gregory (P) owned all of the stock of United Mortgage Corporation, which held 1,000 shares of Monitor Securities Corporation. P formed a new corporation, had United transfer the Monitor shares to the new corporation, and then dissolved it. P now held the Monitor shares and sold them and realized a capital gain. The Commissioner (D) claimed that P received an ordinary income dividend. The Tax Court held for P, but the court of appeals reversed. P appeals.

Issue. Must a valid business purpose be accomplished in effecting a tax-free reorganization?

Held. Yes. Judgment affirmed.

◆   This whole undertaking, though taking on the form of a tax-free reorganization, was nothing more than a devious form of conveyance. A transfer of assets from one corporation to another must be "in pursuance of a plan of reorganization" of corporate business. Here the transfer had no relation to the business of either corporation, but was a mere device to conceal the transaction's real character.

Comment. Note that in this case a corporate reorganization was attempted to afford P the means of transforming ordinary income to capital gain.

---

2. **Ramifications of the Business Purpose Rule.** There are many facets to the "business purpose" doctrine. In addition to the reorganization area, it has had application to many other areas of the tax law. Some of these important aspects:

a. **Sham transactions.** The test is used to disregard the existence or status of an entity that has no purpose other than tax avoidance.

b. **Step transactions.** The business purpose test is used to disregard the separate existence of several steps and instead judge the transaction by its end result. That is, the intervening steps are disregarded, since they lack a business purpose.

c. **Transactions lacking economic reality.** A transaction may involve binding legal obligations more or less permanent in nature (thus, there is no "sham"), and may have an end result complying with statutory requirements (thus, not a "step transaction"), but it may nevertheless lack a business purpose other than its beneficial tax results. These are difficult cases to decide.

   1) Some tax provisions are meant to establish a new business norm based on tax advantages. For example, Western Hemisphere Trade Corporations were created based on tax advantages.

   2) But in other situations, the tax provisions are meant to relate to transactions that do not derive their motivation from the tax law (for example, provisions making a distinction between "debt" and "equity").

J. SALE OF A GOING BUSINESS

1. Introduction--

Williams v. McGowan, 152 F.2d 570 (2d Cir. 1945).

Facts. Williams (P) had a hardware business with a partner who died. P purchased his deceased partner's interest from the estate, and then sold the entire business interest to a third party. He suffered a loss on the transaction, which he reported as ordinary loss on his tax return. The Commissioner (D) determined that the sale of the business qualified as a capital transaction, and assessed P with a tax deficiency. P paid and brought suit in district court, which held for D. P appeals.

Issue. Does the sale of a sole proprietorship result in capital gain or loss?

Held. No. Judgment reversed.

♦ While the sale of a partner's interest is treated as a capital transaction, this business became a sole proprietorship when P bought his partner's interest. No special treatment is accorded to the sale of a sole proprietorship. In defining "capital assets," Congress plainly desired that the sole proprietorship be looked upon as a group of individual assets. In this case, the depreciable fixtures and inventory both fall within exceptions to the capital asset definition. No other sold asset gives rise to capital gain, except possibly the receivables. The case is therefore remanded to determine the nature of the receivables. The remainder of the items are not capital assets.

Dissent. Congress did not intend to carve the sale of a business into separate distinct sales. The parties contracted for the transfer of an entire business. It should be a capital gain or loss.

━━━━━━━━━

2. **Accounts and Notes Receivable.** Section 1221(4) states that an account or note receivable acquired in the ordinary course of business in payment for the taxpayer's services or inventory is not a capital asset.

3. **Goodwill.** Goodwill (the excess of the price a business brings over the market value of the assets) is a capital asset. Therefore, the seller gets capital gain treatment while the buyer does not recover the amount paid for the goodwill until the business is resold or terminated.

K. CORRELATION WITH PRIOR RELATED TRANSACTIONS

1. **Sale of Bad Debts--**

━━━━━━━━━

Merchants National Bank v. Commissioner, 199 F.2d 657 (5th Cir. 1952).

━━━━━━━━━

Facts. Merchants (P) wrote off notes that it determined to be worthless and charged them against ordinary income. Years later P was able to sell the notes for $18,460, which it claimed as a capital gain. The Commissioner (D) and the Tax Court held the receipts to be ordinary income.

Issue. Does the sale of a note which had previously been written off produce a capital gain?

Held. No. Judgment affirmed.

♦ When a deduction for debts deemed worthless is taken, recoveries on the debts in later years constitute taxable income to the extent that a tax benefit was received in the year of deduction. It would be unfair to allow P to reduce its ordinary income fully for the loss of the notes and then attain a capital gain advantage on their subsequent recovery.

━━━━━━━━━

2. The Lookback Rule--

Arrowsmith v. Commissioner, 344 U.S. 6 (1952).

Facts. In 1937, Arrowsmith (P) and the other shareholder decided to liquidate their corporation. Distributions were made in the following four years. P reported the profits as capital gains. In 1944, after the final liquidation, a judgment was rendered against the old corporation which the two previous shareholders were required to pay. P deducted his payment as an ordinary loss. The Commissioner (D) viewed the payment as part of the original liquidation, which would require capital loss treatment. The Tax Court held for P, but the court of appeals reversed. P appeals.

Issue. May transactions of separate tax years be integrated for purposes of classifying one of them as capital or ordinary?

Held. Yes. Judgment affirmed.

♦ Examining related transactions to classify one of them is not an attempt to reopen or readjust a previous tax year. It is apparent that P should not be allowed to receive favorable capital gains treatment on the original distribution, and then claim ordinary loss treatment on payment of the judgment.

Dissent (Douglas, J.). Congress has not authorized the reopening of previous tax years for these purposes. Also, had the liability been paid by the corporation before liquidation, it would have deducted the payment as ordinary loss.

L. REQUIREMENT OF "SALE OR EXCHANGE"

1. **Introduction.** For a transaction to be treated as a capital gain or loss, there must be a sale or exchange. The provisions of sections 1222 and 1231 require that a sale or exchange occur. At times, the courts have confused the "sale or exchange" requirement with the previously discussed "capital asset" requirement. The distinction between the two is not a clear one. In other contexts, courts have ignored the "sale or exchange" requirement, as was done in *Arrowsmith,* where the payment of a judgment was characterized as a capital loss. The courts have usually focused more attention on the status of the asset than on the manner of its disposition.

2. **Forced Sales.** *Helvering v. Hammel,* 311 U.S. 504 (1941), involved the purchase of real estate on an installment land contract. After the purchaser, Hammel, defaulted on his payments, a foreclosure and judicial sale were instituted wherein the vendor reacquired the property and Hammel sustained a $4,000 loss. The Commissioner denied Hammel's ordinary loss deduction, claiming that the loss was derived from a capital asset sale. The Su-

preme Court granted certiorari and held that a forced sale qualifies as a sale or exchange. The Court reasoned that although the land was ordered sold by the court, the act that severed Hammel's rights to the land was its actual sale. This qualifies as a "sale or exchange" as defined in the Code.

3. **Sale or License.** When a franchise, trademark, or tradename is transferred, the question often arises whether the transfer should be treated as a sale (and accorded capital gains treatment) or a license (with the proceeds looked on as ordinary income). Generally, capital gains treatment is allowed only if the transferor did not reserve any significant powers, rights, or continuing interests with respect to the subject matter of the franchise, trademark, or tradename. In the usual franchise, the franchisor retains strict controls over the franchisee's operation. Payments received by the franchisor are ordinary income.

4. **Statutory "Sales or Exchanges."**

   a. **Worthless securities.** When stocks and bonds become worthless, there has been no transaction. The securities still remain in the owner's hands. Nonetheless, section 165(g) states that the loss shall be treated as a sale or exchange on the last day of the tax year in which the security became worthless.

   b. **Loss by fire or condemnation.** Section 1231 treats gains from these (from insurance proceeds) as capital gains, while losses receive an ordinary deduction.

   c. **Retirement of stock.** Section 331 treats amounts paid herein as "in exchange for the stock."

   d. **Purchase and sale by a corporation of its own stock.** It is possible for a corporation to purchase its own stock (known as "treasury stock") and then resell it. Section 1032 provides that a corporation will not recognize any gain or loss when receiving cash or property for its own stock. Also, Rev. Rul. 74-503 states that the basis of treasury stock is zero, regardless of what was given up for the stock.

   e. **Lease cancellation.** Section 1241 provides that when a lessee receives amounts for cancellation of the lease, it is a capital transaction.

TABLE OF CASES
(Page numbers of briefed cases in bold)

NOTES

NOTES

NOTES

NOTES

NOTES

NOTES

NOTES

NOTES